INDIAN
IN 7

Monisha Bharadwaj is an award-winning chef, author and food historian. She was awarded 'Cookery Writer of the Year' by the Guild of Food Writers and her books have been shortlisted for awards such as the André Simon Award, the Cordon Bleu World Food Media Awards and the Jacob's Creek World Food Media Awards. She has written 15 books, including The Indian Cookery Course, which together have sold over half a million copies. Monisha runs her own successful Indian cookery school in London – Cooking with Monisha – teaches once a month at Divertimenti and has recently given demos at Borough Market.

www.cookingwithmonisha.com   @Monishabharadwaj

INDIAN

IN 7

DELICIOUS INDIAN RECIPES IN
7 INGREDIENTS OR FEWER

MONISHA BHARADWAJ

Photography by Gareth Morgans

KYLE BOOKS

This book is for Arrush and India—for being eternally inspiring and for making our kitchen a place of constant laughter and fun!

An Hachette UK Company
www.hachette.co.uk

First published in Great Britain in 2019 by
Kyle Books, an imprint of Kyle Cathie Ltd
Carmelite House
50 Victoria Embankment
London EC4Y 0DZ
www.kylebooks.co.uk

This edition published in 2019.

ISBN: 978 0 857837 769

Distributed in the US by Hachette Book Group,
1290 Avenue of the Americas, 4th and 5th Floors,
New York, NY 10104

Distributed in Canada by Canadian Manda
Group, 664 Annette St., Toronto, Ontario,
Canada M6S 2C8

Publisher: Joanna Copestick
Editor: Vicky Orchard
Editorial assistant: Sarah Kyle
Design: Georgia Vaux
Photography: Gareth Morgans
Food styling: Sunil Vijayakar
Props styling: Hannah Wilkinson
Production: Nic Jones

Printed and bound in China

10 9 8 7 6 5 4 3 2 1

CONTENTS

~

INTRODUCTION

Most people, even those who love Indian food and cook it often, tend to think that it is complicated to make, takes forever, and needs a long list of ingredients to make the dish any good.

An increasing number of people outside of India are now cooking Indian meals at home on a regular basis. With the easy availability of ingredients and disappointment with greasy Indian restaurant food, home cooks are trying their hand at cooking a range of dishes that go beyond the usual takeout fare. Added to this is the fact that as more and more people travel, they are learning about the vast variety of Indian dishes that are as far removed from Chicken Tikka Masala as Dallas is from Delhi.

Although there is this desire to eat fresh, delicious, and healthy food, most people simply do not have the time or energy to create elaborate Indian meals comprising several dishes, or recipes with a long list of ingredients that take time to prepare. Recipes have to be easy and quick to cook in order to appeal to working people, students, and those with busy lives.

This book is certainly not about whittling down the number of ingredients in a traditional recipe just for the sake of a fancy book. There is no doubt that many traditional Indian recipes do call for a lot of ingredients and simply cannot be made without the entire list. I haven't included those sorts of recipes here. However, there are countless dishes that require just a few ingredients and are cooked in many Indian homes each day. Also, newer and better commercially available ingredients than those my grandmother used (such as store-bought garam masala powder or faster-cooking cuts of meat) mean that we need fewer ingredients to work with today.

My own working day is long and I often spend it cooking at my classes and demos. When I get back home tired, cooking another meal is the last thing on my mind, but I still want to create a fresh, homecooked meal that is healthy and delicious and can be rustled up very quickly. For years, I have prepared easy meals from pantry ingredients, such as rice, pasta, oats, and flour, along with quick-cooking fresh vegetables, fish, and meats that are wholesome,

hearty, and extremely satisfying. I have learnt to pre-prepare some ingredients so that cooking a quick meal is not a chore. I often chop some vegetables while having my morning cup of tea and put them in the refrigerator to use later. I always have a tub of ginger-garlic paste that I made earlier in my refrigerator.

There is no doubt that Indian cuisine is complex, given that it is shaped by so many factors, such as climate (which can be so varied in such a vast country), geography, and religious practices, as well as foreign influences that have introduced a huge variety of new ingredients; for example, tomatoes and chilies were introduced by the Portuguese only around 500 years ago. A large number of Indian people are vegetarian; some don't even eat root vegetables as it involves the killing of insects while uprooting them.

Not all Indian food is hot. In places where the climate is hot—for instance, in southern India—food is typically flavored with more chilies so that the capsaicin makes people perspire and cools them down. It is often easy to read a recipe and judge which region it comes from and what religious beliefs and historical events have influenced it.

However, it is a myth that every Indian recipe requires lots of ingredients and processes that take forever to prepare. My biggest challenge in the past few years has been to move my readers away from the misconception that Indian food is greasy, unhealthy, takes hours to prepare, and needs a pantry full of ingredients. In fact, people are keen to try recipes that do not require them to buy an endless array of ingredients that may not be used often and may deteriorate with time.

When I was asked to write this book, I was given the chance to choose three "free" basic ingredients that I could use, as well as up to seven others in the recipes. I chose:

sunflower oil
salt
ginger-garlic paste (simply because they are almost always used together!)—see page 26 for my recipe.

Apart from these three basic ingredients, each recipe uses seven additional ingredients or fewer (this doesn't include any serving suggestions given in the recipes, nor any water used/listed). This will naturally mean shorter preparation and cooking times.

Indian cookery, like many other cuisines, has moved seamlessly into the 21st century so that now people in nuclear families are cooking lighter, healthier meals that are suitable for today's busy lifestyle. Gone are the ghee and cream; cooks have replaced these with light oils and techniques that can create a creamy texture in a healthier way. People in Indian cities are eating simpler meals cooked by men and women who have spent a long day at work and often either live alone, as couples, or in small family groups.

Most of the recipes in this book will serve four people. I have written them with a view that for readers who need only one or two portions, they can take leftovers to work the following day, freeze them, or have them for their next meal!

MEASURES

Although all the recipes in this book have been measured and tested, I believe that the best cooks use a big dose of intuition and judgment. I have found during many years of teaching and demonstrating that however accurate an ingredient list may be, ingredients do vary in size and flavor. Do touch and smell your ingredients, as they cook and when they are ready. They will provide you with the best possible clues about how the dish will turn out.

EQUIPMENT

Pans
Most Indian cooks use a heavy "kadhai" for stir-frying and deep-frying. An Indian kadhai is similar in shape to a Chinese wok, but is heavier as it has to cook food for longer periods of time. You don't need a kadhai for authentic Indian cooking—you can easily use saucepans and frying pans or skillets instead.

Blender/mortar and pestle
An important piece of equipment is the blender, which is needed to make curry pastes and chutneys. I use a large blender for big quantities and a small coffee mill for spice powders and smaller spice blends. Almost every Indian home has a blender—the more powerful, the better, and I'd certainly buy one over 500W. A mortar and pestle is useful to crush spices or small quantities of garlic and ginger.

Knives
A sharp chef's knife that can mince garlic, finely slice onions, or chop fresh cilantro to fine shreds is invaluable. Ensure you keep it sharpened. A sharp knife is much safer than a blunt one, as you'll use far less pressure to chop ingredients and therefore there is less risk of the knife slipping and injuring you.

Cutting boards
I use polyethylene plastic boards as they can go into the dishwasher and are nonporous, and therefore do not hold on to smells such as onion or garlic. Wooden boards are long-lasting but will need regular sanitizing with a kitchen-safe cleaner and proper drying so that they do not become moldy. It's a good idea to have a small selection of colored boards. My kitchen has green and brown for vegetarian food preparation, red for raw meat, and blue for raw fish.

Utensils
You'll need a peeler, grater, spatula, and a reasonable number of wooden or silicone spoons, some slotted and others plain. Ladles are used to scoop up curries and lentil dishes.

Spice tin/box
Although not essential, this is a handy bit of equipment. Every Indian home has this spice tin/box or "masala dabba"—it's most often round, made of stainless steel, and has small bowls that fit snugly inside. Some boxes have a double lid to seal in the freshness.

I like to believe that as an everyday spice box has seven compartments, one surely must not need to use more than seven spices for one's daily cooking! Interestingly, the seven spices in the tin/box may vary from one region of India to another, but a few key spices, such as turmeric, chili, cumin, and coriander, remain the same throughout the country.

If you want to be able to make a quick meal with a few ingredients, it is absolutely essential to stock a go-to kitchen cupboard or pantry that will help cut down on time and effort. Ensure that everything is within date and use up what went in first. Here's what I have in my pantry:

Oil—in this book I have used sunflower oil, but you can use any oil that will heat up to a high temperature without changing its composition, such as vegetable oil, canola oil, or corn oil. I don't use highly flavored oils such as peanut or coconut for everyday cooking as they seem to complement only certain regional recipes.

Canned beans and pulses—such as chickpeas, red kidney beans, lima beans, and black-eyed peas. Remember to rinse them in a strainer under cold water to get rid of excess salt and canning liquid.

Canned fruit—such as pineapple, mango, and mango puree.

Canned peeled chopped tomatoes—you can use whole plum tomatoes but these will need to be chopped, so it's best to buy chopped to save some time. These are invaluable if you want to add color and depth to a dish, because sometimes fresh tomatoes can be lacking in flavor and can also be too watery and pale.

Tomato paste—this is available in cans and tubes and in various sizes. I buy the really deep, double-concentrated ones that are essential to create depth of flavor and color, especially in dishes that depend on this. Opened tubes of paste can be stored in the refrigerator for a couple of weeks. I buy large cans of paste, divide it into plastic tubs and then put these into the freezer. The frozen paste will cut easily with a knife and will last for up to 2 months in the freezer.

Canned coconut milk and coconut powder—check the ingredients on the label for unwanted thickeners, such as guar or xanthan gums. Partly used cans of coconut milk can be decanted into tubs and frozen for later use. I use the full-fat version rather than the reduced-fat or lighter ones, which I find don't give the consistency and richness I'm looking for.

If you require a small amount of coconut milk, it's often impractical to open a can and so I make this with coconut powder or creamed coconut as follows:

> 2 heaped tablespoons coconut powder or creamed coconut (or more, depending on how thick you want the milk to be)
> Scant 1 cup warm water

Combine the coconut powder or creamed coconut with the warm water in a bowl and whisk together until smooth. Use as required.

Nuts—almonds, both whole and sliced, pistachios, cashews, and peanuts. I buy broken cashews for curries—these are cheaper than whole ones and are often blended to a puree to thicken curries and add a creamy texture. When buying peanuts, I get the unsalted ones, but if you have salted peanuts, just wash them before use so that the dish doesn't become too salty.

Brown cane sugar—I use brown sugar whenever I can and when the color of the final dish is not dependent on the sugar being white. I think it has a lovely depth of flavor that complements Indian dishes.

Tamarind—tamarind is a brown, sausage-shaped fruit that grows on large trees. The pod ripens in the summer and the shell becomes brittle. The fruit inside is pulpy and is held together by a fibrous husk. Within this pulp are square, dark brown, shiny seeds that are inedible. It is the pulp that is used for its slightly sweet, very sour taste and fruity aroma. Tamarind is available as a pressed, fibrous slab, or as a jam-like bottled concentrate. As slabs, you can buy "wet" or "dry" tamarind. The wet one is softer to squash and easier to use, whereas the dry one is more difficult to break down.

HOW TO MAKE TAMARIND PULP

¼ block (about 1 ounce) wet tamarind

Put the tamarind in a small bowl with just enough warm water to cover it. Squash the tamarind with your fingers. Once it softens and the water turns brown and thick, pass the mixture through a fine-mesh strainer into a separate bowl. The fine pulp and juice will go through, leaving behind the fibrous husk.

Put some more warm water in the strainer and do a second pressing. You should be able to see the seeds and fibers. Discard these. You can do a couple more pressings until all the pulp has been extracted. You should have 5–6 tablespoons of pulp. The pulp will keep well in an airtight container in the refrigerator for up to 3 weeks.

If all this seems too time-consuming and you need only a small quantity of tamarind, you can buy a jar of tamarind pulp or paste. This is different from and much better than jars of tamarind concentrate, which I find too dark, acidic, and gooey.

SPICES AND SPICE MIXTURES

The aromatic oils in spices are used to impart flavor to cooking. These oils are released in two ways—by heating and by crushing or splitting the spices. This is why spice seeds and spice powders behave differently in the cooking process. The seeds require a higher cooking temperature to split them, whereas the powders need moderate heat to release their oils.

Spice seeds

If the recipe contains oil and seeds, the seeds will always go into the oil first, with the remaining ingredients added on top in a sequence that depends on the time taken for each of them to cook. For example, mustard seeds take longer to pop than cumin seeds, so they go into the pan on their own before the cumin seeds. Seeds are sometimes fried in oil and poured on top of a dish as tempering or "tadka." I simply warm the oil over high heat rather than allowing it to become blazing hot before adding the seeds to the pan. This gives me control as I watch the spice seeds slowly pop or sizzle, rather than fly out of the pan or possibly burn if the oil is too hot.

Toasting spice seeds

Spice seeds are sometimes dry-toasted without any oil and crushed for freshness of flavor. Not all spices need to be crushed every single time you make a meal. The ones that I would recommend be crushed at home are coriander seeds, cumin seeds, and garam masala. Simply put the spice seeds into a dry, cool frying pan, then place the frying pan over high heat to release the seeds' aromatic oils and dry out any residual moisture, making them brittle and easier to crush. As soon as the pan is hot, in a matter of seconds, the seeds will darken and develop an aroma. Tip them into a mortar or a spice mill and crush them to a powder. For the freshest flavor of all, you can put toasted garam masala spices in a pepper mill and, with a few turns each time, sprinkle them on to curries just before serving.

When making a batch of spice powder to store, ensure that the toasted spices are completely cool before crushing or grinding them, otherwise they may become cakey and moldy due to the moisture present in the steam.

Powdered or ground spices

Powdered or ground spices can be added to a dish at three different stages of the cooking process—into the oil at the start of cooking, after having added an ingredient to the pan, such as onions, or as a finishing spice at the end of cooking. The three stages of cooking the spices are:

1. The spices will pop, crackle, or sizzle.
2. They will change color (often lighter spices darken and darker ones lighten slightly).
3. They will develop a cooked aroma.

When cooking spice powders (ground spices) in oil, it is sometimes difficult to estimate exactly when they are "done." You can add a couple of tablespoons of cold water to the pan after the spices have sizzled and allow them to cook for a few minutes until the water has evaporated, leaving the cooked spices in the oil. The aroma will have changed from being quite strong to becoming soft and mellow. Some Indian recipes also ask for spice powders to be mixed into a little cold water and then added to the pan. This allows them to cook without scorching.

These stages progress within seconds when the oil has reached the correct temperature, so ensure you have your next ingredient close at hand. If you have seeds in the pan, you can add any ingredient next, such as onions, tomatoes, chilies, meat, or vegetables. However, if you are cooking spice powders, you will have to add a liquid ingredient as soon as the spices are cooked. This could be tomatoes, tamarind pulp, cooked lentils, or curry pastes.

Most of my recipes ask you to sprinkle in the ground spices on top of ingredients that have reduced the temperature of the pan. For example, the onions go into the oil at the beginning. When they soften enough, the ginger, garlic, and fresh chilies are added. Tomatoes may be next, followed by the spice powders. This way, the temperature in the pan is not high enough to burn the spices, unless, of course, it is left on the heat unattended for too long.

Some spice powders are used as "finishing spices." The usual ones are red chili powder and toasted cumin powder, which are often seen sprinkled on salads, street food called "chaat," and yogurt-based curries. Garam masala is also dusted on to curries for a top note of aroma and warmth.

Turmeric

One of the most traditional and versatile spices used in Indian cooking, turmeric is the heart and soul of any curry. This key ingredient is used daily in every part of India as its unique color—due to the presence of the pigment curcumin—and flavor enrich all regional cuisine. As for the root, only cured turmeric has the aroma and color (chiefly due to the presence of curcumin) necessary for cooking.

Turmeric has an earthy, sensual fragrance and a musky, dry taste, but it is used wholeheartedly in Indian cooking for its wonderful quality of enhancing and balancing the flavors of all the other ingredients. However, be careful not to use too much turmeric when cooking green vegetables as they will turn dull and taste bitter. Be wary when storing and cooking with turmeric as it will stain hands and clothes quite quickly.

Chili powder

Red chili powder is used not only for its heat but also for its color. In curries where a pale color or fresh flavor is required, fresh green chilies are chosen over red chili powder. Many varieties of chilies are bright red but only moderately hot. They are sometimes soaked in water or vinegar and ground to a paste to add a certain color and smokiness to curries. Commercially available chili powder is usually a blend of several varieties and is sold in extra hot, hot, medium, and mild versions. I think it's best to buy the moderate version. I've used Kashmiri chili powder in my recipes.

Interestingly, in India, the bhut jolokia, which has acquired celebrity as one of the world's hottest chilies, is rarely seen outside of the northeastern region where it is grown. In the West, chilies from all over the world, including Thailand and India, are imported and can be seen alongside each other in supermarkets. I use bird's-eye chilies, variously called "long thin" or "thin green" chilies.

Cumin

Cumin seeds are elongated, oval, and long. They range from sage green to tobacco brown in color and have longitudinal ridges. Another variety of cumin is black cumin ("kala jeera," "shahi jeera," or "siya jeera"): the seeds are dark brown to black and are smaller and finer than regular cumin. The smell of cumin is distinctive; it can be described as strong and bitter and is usually loved or hated. Cumin has a warm, somewhat bitter taste.

It is available whole as seeds, or crushed to a powder, which is often blended with ground coriander to form a widely used mixture called "dhana-jeera." This combination is one of the essential spice blends used in Indian cuisine. Toasted cumin powder (see Toasting Spice Seeds on page 12) gives a lift to many curries and yogurt-based raitas or salads.

Coriander/cilantro

Cilantro is the most commonly used garnish in Indian cuisine, and adds a dewy-green touch to red or brown curries. The dried seeds of the plant are the spice. Coriander is perhaps one of the first spices known to man and has been around for over 3,000 years.

Cilantro leaves and coriander seeds are completely different with regards to aroma and flavor. The fresh leaves (and stems) taste and smell fresh and fruity with a hint of ginger. The dried seeds, on the other hand, have a sweet aroma with a subtle whiff of pine and pepper. Bunches of fresh cilantro are commonly available at grocery stores and supermarkets. It looks quite like parsley, but the test lies in the aroma—parsley has a more delicate smell than cilantro.

Mustard seeds

There are three main varieties of mustard seeds: yellow, and the ones used in Indian cooking—brown and black—which are pretty much interchangeable. Raw mustard seeds have almost no smell, but on cooking they acquire a distinctive, acrid, baked-earth aroma that dominates any dish. The seeds are sharp,

nutty, slightly bitter, and aromatic in taste. Their heat is often misjudged, so be careful when adding them to recipes.

Commercially blended mustards are not used in Indian cooking but they can make a reasonable substitute for homemade mustard paste. In south India and along the coast, mustard is used primarily as tempering. In Bengal, mustard seeds are crushed to a paste for use in fiery marinades and curries.

Garam masala

Some of the most expensive spices go into the making of garam masala (literally "warming spices"), and there are as many recipes for it as there are households in India. Depending on individual taste, the proportions of the various ingredients can be adjusted to make this an aromatic rather than a hot blend. I have created my blend (see right) using spices for aroma (cardamom, cinnamon, fennel), as well as for bulking and thickening curries (coriander, cumin). I keep away from recipes that have a long list of ingredients as some garam masala mixes do, and find that this recipe is sufficiently aromatic.

Garam masala is used whole or ground depending on what's cooking. The basic blend includes cloves, cinnamon, cardamom, peppercorns, bay leaves, mace, cumin seeds, and coriander seeds. Commercially bought garam masala is quite good if used within a couple of months. The blend is easy to grind at home, so it is best to buy whole, plump spices and crush them in an electric grinder, coffee mill or using a mortar and pestle. This mixture can then be stored in an airtight container in a cool, dark place for up to 6 months.

Garam masala can be added at different stages of cooking for different degrees of flavor. It is also used as a finishing spice. You can make a larger batch of garam masala by doubling or tripling the spices listed below.

Makes around 1¾ oz

1 teaspoon black peppercorns
2 teaspoons cumin seeds
¾-inch piece of cinnamon stick
10 green cardamom pods, seeds removed and
  husks discarded
5 black cardamom pods, seeds removed and
  husks discarded
10 cloves
3 dried bay leaves
2 blades of mace
1 teaspoon fennel seeds
2 teaspoons coriander seeds

Heat a dry frying pan over medium heat, add all the spices and dry-toast until they start to darken and become aromatic. Remove from the heat and let cool completely before grinding to a fine powder in a spice mill or using a mortar and pestle. Store in an airtight container in a cool, dark place and consume within 6 months.

If stored properly, away from heat, light, air and moisture, spice seeds will last up to a year. Powders and powdered spice blends should ideally be used within 6 months.

OTHER SPICES AND INGREDIENTS THAT I COMMONLY USE

Cinnamon

The dried bark of the cinnamon tree is the spice used in cooking. I use cinnamon sticks for biryanis and curry pastes as they have a more powerful flavor than store-bought ground cinnamon. Not all recipes call for cinnamon and it's not one of the everyday spices in Indian cooking. When used, it is often added whole into curries or rice, so it's best to crush the sticks using a mortar and pestle as and when needed. It is also an essential part of the standard blend of garam masala.

Green cardamom

This is one of the most expensive spices in the world. The fat, green pods grown in Kerala, south India, are considered the best. Cardamom pods are oval capsules containing hard, dark brown seeds that are sticky and cling together. The outer husk is chewy and inedible. I always bruise the pods, extract and crush the seeds to use, and discard the husks. This gives a lovely aroma to the dish and one does not have to deal with biting into whole pods unexpectedly!

Asafoetida (hing)

Although not native to India, asafoetida has for centuries been an essential part of Indian cuisine and medicine. Asafoetida is the dried latex from the rhizomes of several species of ferula or giant fennel. It is grown chiefly in Iran and Afghanistan, from where it is exported to the rest of the world.

Asafoetida has a pungent, unpleasant smell quite like that of pickled eggs, due to the presence of sulfur compounds. This pungency reduces when the spice is cooked and it acquires an aroma like that of cooked onions and garlic. Its powerful smell complements lentils, vegetables, and pickles. It is often used as a digestive spice in vegetarian cooking and in place of garlic in the cuisines of some religions, such as Jainism, which forbid the use of garlic or any ingredient grown underground as it could lead to the destruction of life when they are uprooted. Asafoetida is always used in small quantities—a pinch added to hot oil before the other ingredients is enough to flavor a dish for four people.

Mango powder (amchoor)

This is made from raw, sour, green mangoes, especially windfalls or wild mangoes. The unripe fruits are peeled, cut into thin slices, dried, and powdered to make a fruity, sour spice that is used as a souring agent, especially in dry recipes that would change by the addition of a wet ingredient. Amchoor is available in specialty supermarkets in the West and can be substituted with lemon juice.

Pepper

In India, black pepper is used in every type of regional cooking, often as part of a garam masala blend. It can be cooked with the main ingredients or sprinkled on top as a finishing spice.

Ajowan (ajwain)

This is a close relative of dill, caraway, and cumin. The fragrance of the spice is very similar to that of oregano. Ajowan goes particularly well with green beans and root vegetables, and in dishes that are flour-based, all of which form an important part of India's vast vegetarian cuisine. Snacks like Bombay mix and onion bhajias depend on spices like ajowan for their unique flavor.

Saffron

Today India and Spain are the only major producers of this spice. In India, it only grows in the valley of Kashmir. Saffron is the dried stigmas of the *Crocus sativus*, a perennial bulb, that flowers for just 2 weeks in late October. In India, the lavender-blue blossoms are plucked at dawn before the hot sun wilts them. Then the delicate stigmas are prised out from within each flower and dried artificially or in the sun.

Saffron is made up of fine, orange-gold threads that are so light that 750,000 handpicked flowers yield only about 1 pound. When fresh, saffron is bright and glossy, but exposure to light and air makes it dull and brittle. Pure saffron is believed to be able to color and flavor 70,000 times its weight in liquid. Its intense, musky aroma suffuses the dish to which it has been added and the taste is delicate and only very slightly bitter. It is the most expensive spice in the world due to its scarcity, fragility, and flavor. That is why the temptation to adulterate it is considerable. The usual

adulterant is safflower, aptly called "bastard saffron." Cheaper and with thicker strands than saffron, it will turn food golden but will not flavor it.

Saffron enhances savory food as well as sweet. A few strands soaked in a little warm water or milk and added to a dish along with the liquid add a fragrant richness. It especially complements milk desserts, rice pulaos, and biryanis, as well as white meats such as fish and chicken.

Curry leaves

The whole plant, including the stems, has a strong curry-like odor. The taste is slightly bitter but pleasant and aromatic. Curry leaves are available fresh, frozen, or dried. Fresh leaves have a beautiful fragrance that is partially lost on drying or freezing. If you have a bunch of fresh curry leaves, these can be home-dried for later use: simply spread the bunch out on a tray, stalks and all, and dry for 2–3 days at room temperature. Discard the stalks and store the leaves in an airtight container in the refrigerator for up to 3 months. I find this a better way to retain their flavor than freezing them. Commercially bought curry leaves almost always lack flavor.

Basmati rice

This variety of rice, grown in the foothills of the Himalayas, is the one most seen in stores outside India. In India, people eat locally grown rice varieties that are unique to that particular region.

When buying basmati rice, choose one that has been aged (it may say aged, mature, or old on the pack, or the price will be an indicator—aged rice is more expensive than non-aged rice). Very good-quality basmati is left to age and mature for 1½–2 years in large warehouses in controlled conditions of moisture, light, and temperature. Old rice has a better chance of cooking into separate grains, whereas new rice can become sticky when cooked.

Flours

Atta is a stoneground wholewheat flour that is used to make rotis and parathas. It cannot be substituted with all-purpose flour, chickpea flour, or besan for pancakes and for thickening.

Various lentils

Lentils are called "dal" in many parts of India. They are essentially carbohydrate and protein with no fat. India is one of the largest growers of lentils in the world because of ideal climatic conditions as well as the high demand for them.

Dal is the staple food all over India and is eaten with rice or rotis. The word "dal" is quite confusing because it is loosely used for a large group of lentils, pulses, and legumes, both cooked and uncooked. Every Indian food store I have been to has had quite a few shelves stacked with legumes. Indian dals are available in three main forms:

Whole pulse (sabut dal)—this is the whole bean, as in mung bean (green), urad/urid bean (black), or masoor (brown lentils), so will be called, for example, "sabut mung ki dal."

Split pulse (chilka)—this is the split bean with the skin on, such as mung dal chilka.

Hulled pulse (dhuli hui dal)—this is the split, skinned bean, such as mung dal (these are yellow when the green skin is stripped away), urad dal (when the black skin is removed, the lentil within is creamy white), or masoor dal (red lentils which are inside the brown skin).

Red/orange lentils (masoor dal)

Orange lentils are the seeds of a bushy plant and grow in long pods. When left whole, the lentils are dark brown to greenish-black in color, round and flattish. The fairly thick skin conceals a pinkish-orange center. These lentils are delicate in flavor and have a nutty, fresh taste. The whole lentils are muskier, chewier, and coarser than the skinned lentils.

Three kinds of yellow lentils

Mung (moong) beans or green gram, are very versatile. "Bean sprouts," commonly available everywhere, are actually sprouted mung beans. Whole mung beans, or green gram, are small, oval, and olive green in color. When split, they are small, flattish, and yellow. Whole mung beans have a stronger flavor and texture than the split ones. They are rather chewy and musky. The yellow split mung beans are extremely easy to cook, need no soaking, and are easy to digest.

Pigeon pea (toor or arhar dal)

In some parts of India, yellow lentils are slightly oiled to increase their shelf life, more so when the lentils are exported, and therefore Indian stores outside India usually stock the oily variety of yellow lentils as well as the non-oily ones.

Gram lentils (chana dal), or Bengal gram (as it is also known)

This is the most widely grown lentil in India. They are husked and left whole, split, or ground into a flour called besan. This flour is used to make batter (as in fritters), or as a thickening agent in curries, or it is cooked with jaggery to make many different sweets.

Urad dal

This is also known as black lentil or gram and is the same size and shape as the mung bean. It has an earthy flavor and, when cooked, develops a creamy, slippery texture that is prized in some recipes.

COMMON INGREDIENTS USED IN THE RECIPES IN THIS BOOK

Onions

As a general rule, I have mainly used regular onions in the recipes. I find that red onions can be too sweet for most curries, so I tend to use them when I want a particularly caramelized flavor.

How to cook onions for a curry

The first step is to cut all your ingredients evenly—this will ensure even cooking. I have found that the best way to minimize the crying when cutting onions is to put them in the refrigerator for a little while before chopping them. This seems to stabilize the sulfur oils. Also, not disturbing the root too much helps—when slicing onions, cut off the root, and while dicing, cut around it, discarding some of the flesh. When slicing onions, work along the grain or the fine lines that you see on the onion. This helps the slices to cook evenly. The secret of many curries is to cook the onions well

at the beginning. Some curries need the onions to be blended into a paste—I have found that cooking the onions first helps to bring out their flavor better than blending them raw and then cooking the paste. If you want color in your curry, the onions will have to be shallow-fried.

Start them in a good splash of sunflower oil over high heat, sprinkling in a pinch of salt to hasten the cooking. When they begin to brown, reduce the heat to medium and continue cooking for 7–8 minutes until they are very soft and you can insert a knife into a piece of onion easily. In recipes where you do not want color, the sliced onions can be boiled in just enough water to cover them.

When the onions are not to be pureed, cook them until soft but not as long as above because they will continue cooking with the remaining ingredients.

Chilies

I prefer to use the thin, fresh green chilies that are sold as bird's-eye chilies. I don't scrape the seeds out to reduce the heat, instead I just use a lower number of chilies—you can leave them out completely, if you prefer. Fresh red chilies are green chilies that have ripened. As they will have a shorter storage life when you bring them home, people often prefer to buy the green ones.

Potatoes

I'm often asked which potatoes to use for a particular dish—I prefer waxy ones, such as Charlotte or Anya, for their ability to hold their shape, but I often use floury ones, such as russet or King Edwards, when making mashed potato or in curries where a bit of potato breakdown adds to the thickening of the sauce.

ADRAK-LASAN
Ginger-garlic Paste

Ginger and garlic are often used together in Indian cooking. To buy ginger that is fresh, ensure the skin is firm, shiny, and pale brown in color. This thin skin can be easily scraped off with a teaspoon.

1 part fresh ginger, skin scraped off and flesh chopped
2 parts garlic, peeled and chopped (by volume)

Combine the ginger and garlic. If you are making a small amount, you can grate both or crush them using a mortar and pestle. You don't need to discard the green "soul" from the center of the garlic; it is edible and any bitterness it has will add to the balance of flavors in the overall dish.

If making a larger amount, whiz the peeled and chopped ginger and garlic in a blender, along with a little cold water to turn the blades, and make a smooth paste.

You can store this paste in the refrigerator or freezer. Put it into a clean jam jar, top it up with oil (any cooking oil) and put it in the refrigerator. It will keep in the refrigerator for up to 3 weeks. You will find that the oil layer may decrease with each scoop of paste used—just top it up as necessary.

To freeze the paste, either put it into ice-cube trays, cover it with plastic wrap and store in the freezer for up to 3 months, or put it into a freezer bag, lay this on a metal tray and freeze it flat. Once frozen, it becomes quite brittle and you can snap off as much as you need for each recipe. While ginger-garlic cubes need thawing, the bits broken off from a flat sheet can be added directly to the pan.

CHAVAL
Plain Boiled Rice

ABSORPTION METHOD

I use this method of cooking rice if it's flavored with spices, such as in a pulao or a biryani. When the exact amount of water is added to rice, there is no need to drain it away and thereby all the flavor is retained. Use the best quality, aged basmati (see page 23) for this method as an unaged rice may become sticky.

Serves 4

1¼ cups basmati rice, washed and drained
1¾ cups cold water
4 pinches of salt (optional)

Put the rice, cold water, and salt (if using) into a heavy-based saucepan and bring to a boil without stirring. Reduce the heat to the lowest setting, stir once, gently, and then cover the pan with a tight-fitting lid.

Simmer for 10 minutes, without lifting the lid, then remove from the heat and leave the rice to rest for 5 minutes, covered.

Remove the lid, gently run a fork through the rice to loosen it, and serve hot.

DRAINING METHOD

This is a good way of cooking rice when you have many dishes on the go. You can use this method with brown or wholegrain basmati rice, but the cooking time will be longer—allow 30–45 minutes simmering time.

Serves 4

1¼ cups basmati rice, washed and drained
2½ cups boiling water
4 pinches of salt (optional)

Put the rice, boiling water, and salt (if using) into a saucepan and bring to a boil. Stir once, gently, then reduce the heat to a simmer and cook until the rice is done. This can take 10–12 minutes, depending on your pan and heat source.

Partially covering your pan will cook the rice faster. You can test the rice by squashing a grain between your thumb and forefinger or simply by tasting it.

Drain the rice through a strainer, allowing all the water to drain away. Serve hot.

VARIATIONS

Add ½ teaspoon ground turmeric to the water at the start of cooking.
Add 1 teaspoon cumin seeds to the water at the start of cooking.
Add a handful of frozen garden peas to the water at the start of cooking.
Add a cinnamon stick or a couple of star anise to the water at the start of cooking.

ROTIS/CHAPATIS
Unleavened Flatbreads

Rotis or chapatis are essentially the same thing and are considered everyday bread in India as they are healthy. They are made with wholewheat flour, they're easy to prepare, and you can vary the thickness depending on what they are meant to scoop up—thicker for thick lentils and meats, and thinner for dry vegetable dishes. Some cooks add a tablespoonful of plain yogurt to the dough to make it softer, in which case, the water required will be less.

Makes 10 rotis

2 cups stoneground wholewheat flour (atta),
  plus extra for dusting
2/3–3/4 cup tepid water
sunflower oil, for brushing (optional)

Put the flour in a bowl and, using your fingers, gradually mix in the tepid water until you have a pliable dough. Knead on a lightly floured surface for 5–8 minutes (the more you knead the dough, the softer the rotis), then leave the dough to rest in the bowl for 10 minutes, covered with a clean, damp dish towel.

Divide the dough into 10 equal-size portions, each the size of a small lime. Coat each portion lightly with flour, shape into a ball in your palm, and flatten slightly.

Roll each ball out into a flat disk, 4½ inches in diameter, dusting the surface with flour as necessary.

Heat a griddle pan or shallow frying pan on high heat. Fry the disks, one at a time, on the griddle until the surface appears bubbly. Flip over and press the edges down with a clean cloth or spatula to cook evenly. As soon as the roti is opaque and flecked with brown spots, it is done. Ensure that the roti is cooked evenly all over. Remove the roti and brush with sunflower oil (if using). Cook all the rotis in the same way.

Once each roti is cooked, wrap in a clean dish towel to keep warm while the other rotis are being cooked.

FRESH

GOBI KE CHAVAL
Minted Cauliflower Rice with Green Pepper

Cauliflower grated into rice-like grains is an ideal way to enjoy Indian flavors without the carbs and calories that rice has. When I first made cauliflower rice, I realized how filling and satisfying it can be if flavored well. Best of all, it takes only a few minutes to cook. Ensure you stir it frequently while cooking to keep it fluffy, otherwise it can form clumps. If you'd like a bit of heat in this dish, add a couple of chopped chilies after the cumin seeds have darkened. Fry them for a few seconds and then add the green pepper.

Serves 4

½ head of cauliflower, coarsely grated or processed into "rice" in a food-processor	1 teaspoon cumin seeds	1 green pepper, cored, seeded, and finely chopped	a small handful of mint, leaves picked (woody stalks discarded) and finely chopped	squeeze of fresh lemon juice

Tip the cauliflower "rice" into a bowl, season with salt, and let stand for 10 minutes. Squeeze the cauliflower in a strainer to get rid of as much juice as possible.

Heat 1 tablespoon sunflower oil in a saucepan and add the cauliflower "rice." Stir constantly on high heat for 5 minutes or until it begins to darken slightly in color. Remove from the heat, tip into a bowl, and set aside.

Warm another tablespoon of sunflower oil in the same pan, add the cumin seeds and cook on high heat until they darken, then add the green pepper and stir-fry on high heat for 5–6 minutes, until soft.

Mix in the cauliflower "rice" and mint. Adjust the seasoning to taste and drizzle with the lemon juice.

Serve with a salad and some plain yogurt.

ZUKINI SUVA KI SUBZI
Dilled Zucchini with Fennel Seeds

Dill leaves are used as a vegetable in Indian home cooking but are rarely seen on restaurant menus. Its strong taste can put some people off—if you're one of them, swap the dill for fresh cilantro or spinach. Asafoetida, a strong-smelling powdered spice that adds a garlicky note to a dish, is also added to food as it's known to be a digestive. The sulfuric aroma means that it smells better cooked than raw. Be careful not to add too much—a large pinch is enough for four people; too much and it can easily overpower the dish. If you cannot buy asafoetida easily, leave it out of this dish.

Serves 4

1 teaspoon fennel seeds	¼ teaspoon asafoetida	2 large zucchini (with the skins left on), diced	1 teaspoon ground turmeric	1 teaspoon ground coriander	a handful of dill leaves (thick stems discarded), chopped	squeeze of fresh lemon juice

Warm 2 tablespoons of sunflower oil in a saucepan, add the fennel seeds, and cook on high heat until they darken slightly, then add the asafoetida.

Add the zucchini and mix well, then stir in the turmeric and coriander. Mix well and cook on high heat for 2–3 minutes.

Add the dill leaves and season with salt, then add 2–3 tablespoons of cold water. Cook on high heat until the mixture sizzles, then reduce the heat, cover, and cook until the zucchini are soft and no water remains in the pan.

Finish with the lemon juice and serve hot with Rotis (see page 28).

VANGYACHE BHARIT
Fire-roasted Eggplant with Red Onion and Yogurt

If you have a gas stovetop, you can cook the eggplant directly on the gas flame as it gets a lovely, smoky flavor that you can't get if you oven-bake it. Use a pair of tongs to turn it every minute or so—it should take about 8 minutes to cook, depending on the thickness and size of the eggplant. This smoky eggplant is cooked with different spices and flavorings around India—this a Maharashtrian dish with the addition of locally grown peanuts.

Serves 4

1 large eggplant	1 large red onion, finely chopped	2 fresh green chilies, finely chopped (seeds and all)	1 tomato, finely chopped	1 tablespoon chopped fresh cilantro leaves	generous 1 cup Greek yogurt	2 tablespoons roasted peanuts (salted or unsalted), crushed

Preheat the broiler to high.

Brush the eggplant with 1 tablespoon of sunflower oil and place on a rack under the broiler, ensuring that you put the broiler pan underneath to collect the juice. Turn from time to time until the eggplant is soft and the skin is crispy and dry. Alternatively, cook it directly over a gas flame for about 8 minutes.

Let the eggplant cool slightly, then peel off the skin—it should come off easily. Mash the eggplant flesh in a bowl with a fork until there are no long strands. Set aside.

Heat 1 tablespoon of sunflower oil in a frying pan and fry the onion on high heat until it starts to turn golden, about 3 minutes. Add the chilies, then reduce the heat and cook for 6–7 minutes, until you can cut through a piece of onion easily. Add the tomato and cook for a couple of minutes to soften.

Remove from the heat. Season with salt and stir in the cilantro, then mix in the mashed eggplant. Scoop the mixture into a bowl and let cool for 10 minutes, then finish it off by stirring in the yogurt. Sprinkle the peanuts on top.

Serve cold as a dip with pita breads or naans.

MAKKAI KUMBH KI SUBZI
Sweet Corn and Mushroom Curry

This north Indian dish is a quick and easy meal that can be made more substantial by the addition of some leftover cooked meat or potatoes. Grating tomatoes is an easy way to make a fresh puree without the hassle of blanching them in boiling water. Ripe, slightly soft tomatoes are easier to grate than very firm ones. I like the chewy texture and earthiness of chestnut mushrooms, but you can try other varieties, such as oyster, if you prefer.

Serves 4

3 large tomatoes	1 teaspoon cumin seeds	thumb-size piece of fresh ginger, skin scraped off and flesh finely grated	1 teaspoon Kashmiri chili powder	2 teaspoons garam masala	1¾ cups frozen or canned corn	10 white or chestnut mushrooms, cleaned and thickly sliced

Cut each tomato in half, then grate the cut sides on the large holes of a grater. Discard the skin.

Warm 2 tablespoons of sunflower oil in a heavy-based saucepan and fry the cumin seeds on high heat until they turn slightly dark and aromatic.

Stir in the ginger and fry for 30 seconds. Sprinkle in the ground spices and cook for a few seconds, then add 3 tablespoons of cold water, reduce the heat to low and cook for a further minute, or until the water has evaporated, leaving the spices in oil. Add the grated tomatoes and cook on high heat for 4–5 minutes.

Tip in the corn and mushrooms, season with salt and bring to a boil, then reduce the heat and simmer for a couple of minutes.

Serve warm with Rotis (see page 28) or pita breads.

MASALA TIKKI
Spicy Vegetable Cutlets

In India, a cutlet is not a thin cut of meat as in the West, it refers to a mix of ground meat or mashed vegetables coated with flour, breadcrumbs, or semolina and then fried. Cutlets are usually eaten as a snack but can make a light lunch or a more filling meal if served with some plain yogurt and salad.

Makes 8 cutlets

☸	☸	☸	☸	☸	☸	☸
2 fresh green chilies, finely chopped (seeds and all)	1 teaspoon ground turmeric	1 teaspoon amchoor (dried mango powder) or 1 tablespoon fresh lemon juice	1 carrot, peeled and coarsely grated	a handful of green beans, washed and very finely diced	3 large boiled potatoes (with their skins on), cooled	1 cup fine semolina

Heat 1 tablespoon of sunflower oil in a saucepan, add the chilies, and cook on high heat until they start to sizzle, then add the turmeric and amchoor (if using lemon juice, stir this into the mashed potatoes later on). When the spices start to sizzle, add the grated carrot and green beans. Season with salt, mix well, and cook for a minute. Pour in 4 tablespoons of cold water, bring to a boil, then reduce the heat, cover, and simmer until the water has evaporated.

Meanwhile, peel the potatoes, then mash in a bowl. Stir in the cooked vegetable mixture (and lemon juice, if using), and adjust the seasoning to taste.

Heat enough sunflower oil to liberally cover the base of a large frying pan and set it on high heat. Shape the potato mixture into eight round, flat cakes or cutlets, then dip each one in the semolina to coat all over, shaking off the excess.

Shallow-fry the cutlets, four at a time, for 4–5 minutes, until golden brown on each side, flipping them over once halfway through the cooking time. Remove and drain on paper towels. Cover with foil to keep warm while you cook the remaining cutlets. Serve hot.

ELUMICHAI SADAM
Fragrant Lime Rice

South India is essentially rice eating and there are countless rice recipes flavored with local ingredients. This is one of my favorite recipes—the golden color of the rice, the tangy flavor and tantalizing citrussy aroma of lime, and the crunch of the nuts make this a hero dish when I'm entertaining. Where it comes from, this dish is served on festive occasions. You can use lemon or lime to give it a fresh, summery aroma. The coconut adds another layer of texture and can also be chopped up into small pieces and folded into the rice along with the lime zest.

Serves 4

1¼ cups basmati rice, washed and drained	1 teaspoon mustard seeds	10 cashews	2 tablespoons unsalted peanuts	1 teaspoon ground turmeric	zest and juice of 1 large lime	fresh coconut slices, to garnish

Put the rice and 2½ cups boiling water into a heavy-based saucepan and season with salt. Bring to a boil, then reduce the heat, stir once and simmer for 8–9 minutes until a grain can be easily mashed between your fingers. Drain through a colander and set aside.

Warm 1 tablespoon of sunflower oil in a frying pan and fry the mustard seeds on high heat until they start to pop. Add the cashews and peanuts and reduce the heat. When the cashews are slightly brown, add the turmeric and cook for a few seconds, then pour in the lime juice. Gently fold the rice and lime zest into this mixture.

Serve hot, garnished with a sprinkling of coconut slices, with some plain yogurt and hot lime pickle on the side.

MUTTAR PANEER
Paneer with Peas

Paneer is Indian cottage cheese—it's made by splitting whole milk into cheese and whey with the use of an acid, such as lemon juice. It is dense, easily available commercially, and is unsalted and bland, so that it can absorb the flavors of the spices it is cooked with. It does not melt, so when cooking it, look for a softening—from being quite firm, on heating, it will become spongy. Some cooks fry paneer in oil before adding it to curries, mainly for a rich golden color and a chewy texture. I prefer it un-fried as it remains softer.

Serves 4

1–2 fresh green chilies, slit in half lengthwise and stalks left on	1 teaspoon dried fenugreek leaves	2 tablespoons tomato paste	1 teaspoon ground turmeric	1 teaspoon ground cumin	2½ cups frozen garden peas	9 ounces paneer, cubed

Warm 2 tablespoons of sunflower oil in a saucepan on high heat and fry the chilies until they begin to sizzle. Crumble in the fenugreek leaves.

Add the tomato paste and fry for 30 seconds, then add the turmeric and cumin. Fry for a few seconds, then add a splash of cold water and cook for a minute, still on high heat.

Add the peas and season with salt. Add a scant ½ cup of cold water and cook until the peas are tender, about 8 minutes (adding a little more water, if necessary). The curry should have a thick sauce that coats the peas. Fold in the paneer and simmer for a couple of minutes. Serve hot with Rotis (see page 28).

BHINDI KI KADHI
Okra in a Delicate Yogurt Curry

Yogurt curry is made in every region of India, in many forms. In the north, texture is provided by the addition of little flour dumplings called "pakode"; in Gujarat, it is made with an assortment of vegetables, including okra; and in the south, this curry is made fragrant with spices. Here, gram flour or "besan" is used for thickening—it's made from a pulse called Bengal gram and is gluten free. It cannot be substituted with all-purpose flour.

Serves 4

1⅓ cups plain yogurt	3 tablespoons gram flour	1 teaspoon black mustard seeds	1–2 fresh green chilies (depending on how hot you like it), finely chopped (seeds and all)	1 teaspoon finely grated peeled fresh ginger	1 teaspoon ground turmeric	5½ ounces okra, tops cut off and each one cut in half

Combine the yogurt and gram flour in a large bowl. Slowly add about 2 cups of cold water, whisking all the time to remove any lumps. Add enough water to make a soupy, pouring consistency. Set aside.

Warm 2 tablespoons of sunflower oil in a heavy-based saucepan, add the mustard seeds and cook on high heat until they begin to pop, then add the chilies, ginger, and turmeric and cook for a few seconds.

Add the okra, season with salt, and stir. Cook on high heat for 2–3 minutes, then reduce the heat and cook for a further 6–7 minutes, stirring from time to time, until you can easily pierce a knife through a piece of okra.

Pour in the yogurt mixture, stirring frequently to prevent lumps forming. When the mixture is almost boiling, reduce the heat and cook on low heat until it thickens, about 10 minutes.

Taste the curry to check that it has lost the raw flour flavor, then adjust the seasoning to taste.

Serve hot with plain boiled rice and poppadoms.

BATATYACHI BHAJI
Mumbai-style Potatoes

Bombay aloo, a popular dish on Indian takeout menus in Britain, is not to be found in Mumbai (formerly Bombay), but this recipe comes from the local Mumbai people, the Maharashtrians, whose cuisine is simple and yet full of flavor. This is eaten on festive days, along with fried bread for breakfast, or as part of a family meal. Some cooks add a tablespoon of crushed peanuts at the end, which gives this dish a unique fragrance and texture.

Serves 4

3 large potatoes, peeled, washed, and cut into ½-inch cubes	2 large tomatoes	1 teaspoon brown or black mustard seeds	pinch of asafoetida	2 fresh green chilies, finely chopped (seeds and all)	1 teaspoon ground turmeric	a small handful of fresh cilantro leaves, chopped

Put the potatoes into a heavy-based saucepan, cover with boiling water, and season with salt. Bring to a boil, then reduce the heat and simmer until the potatoes are just cooked, which means that each cube is cooked through but still holds its shape, about 15 minutes. Drain and set aside.

Cut each tomato in half, then grate the cut sides on the large holes of a grater. Discard the skin.

Warm 1 tablespoon of sunflower oil in a separate saucepan and fry the mustard seeds on high heat until they begin to pop. Add the asafoetida and chilies, then stir in the tomatoes. Bring to a boil, then reduce the heat, stir in the turmeric, and cook for 30 seconds.

Add the cooked potatoes. Turn up the heat, adjust the salt to taste, and stir to mix. Don't worry if the potatoes disintegrate a bit, they are meant to! Add the cilantro, mix lightly, then remove from the heat and serve hot.

PUDINA PULAO

Mint Pulao

This lovely green rice dish can be served simply with some yogurt mixed with grated cucumber and seasoned with salt and black pepper. I add a good sprinkling of nuts on top before serving for a bit of crunch and texture. You can add any green vegetables to the blend along with the mint—try a handful of kale or spinach, a few slices of seeded green pepper, or some fresh cilantro leaves. Another option is to add some colorful vegetables with the rice—I like carrots, red or yellow peppers, and garden peas.

Serves 4

a large handful of mint leaves (woody stalks discarded), chopped	2–3 fresh green chilies (depending on how hot you like it), finely chopped (seeds and all)	1 teaspoon cumin seeds	1¼ cups basmati rice, washed and drained	2 tablespoons toasted nuts (try pine nuts, sliced almonds, or salted peanuts), to garnish

Put the mint and chilies into a blender and add scant 1 cup of cold water to turn the blades. Blend to a fine puree. Pour this into a measuring cup and add enough cold water to make up to 1¾ cups. Set aside.

Warm 1 tablespoon of sunflower oil in a heavy-based saucepan on high heat, add the cumin seeds and fry until they darken and release an aroma, then add 1 teaspoon of Ginger-garlic Paste (see page 26) and fry for 30 seconds.

Tip in the rice, season with salt, and then pour in the mint and chili mixture. Bring to a boil, stir once, then reduce the heat to an absolute minimum, cover, and simmer for 12 minutes without lifting the lid.

Turn off the heat and leave the rice to rest for 5 minutes. Remove the lid and fluff up the rice with a fork. Serve hot, sprinkled with the toasted nuts.

PARSNIP AUR GAJAR KI SUBZI
Curried Parsnips and Carrots

Parsnips are not seen in India but seem to lend themselves very well to Indian spices. Try this recipe by swapping the parsnips for mixed peppers in the summer. I have added quinoa to this recipe, as I sometimes have this dish on its own as a light lunch and the quinoa provides texture and protein. I soak the quinoa for 10 minutes before cooking it as this takes away the outer skins, which can be bitter. As this dish can be reheated or eaten cold, it makes an excellent packed lunch to take to work or school.

Serves 4

2 tablespoons quinoa	1 teaspoon black or brown mustard seeds	1 teaspoon ground turmeric	1 teaspoon ground cumin	3 parsnips, peeled and chopped	2 carrots, peeled and chopped

Soak the quinoa in a bowl of boiling hot water for 10 minutes, then drain in a strainer and rinse well under cold water. Put the quinoa into a small saucepan along with scant ⅔ cup of cold water. Bring to a boil, then reduce the heat and simmer for 10–12 minutes, until all the water has been absorbed. Remove from the heat, fluff up with a fork, and set aside.

Warm 2 tablespoons of sunflower oil in a separate saucepan on high heat, add the mustard seeds and when they pop, add the turmeric and cumin. After a few seconds, add a couple of tablespoons of cold water and cook on medium heat until the water has evaporated, leaving the spices in oil.

Tip in the vegetables and season with salt. Pour in a scant ½ cup of cold water and bring to a boil, then cover and cook on medium heat for 15–20 minutes, until the vegetables are soft but still hold their shape. You may need to add a few tablespoons of cold water if the pan dries out and the vegetables are still uncooked. Stir in the reserved quinoa until its is warmed through.

Serve hot with Rotis (see page 28) or a side salad.

COMFORT

MURGH TIKKA

Tandoori-style Baked Chicken Tikka

The word "tikka," often misunderstood as a "sauce" or a "tandoori-cooked food," especially outside of India, actually means a dice-cut of chicken breast, usually about 1 inch in size. Chicken tikka served with plain couscous and grilled vegetables (I like zucchini, eggplant, and mixed peppers) is an all-time favorite meal in my home. In this recipe, make sure you add the oil after you've added the spices and salt, otherwise, it will create a barrier and not allow the spices to permeate through the chicken. The cooked tikka can also be cooled, shredded, and mixed into a cold salad.

Serves 4

2 teaspoons Kashmiri chili powder	1 teaspoon ground turmeric	1 teaspoon ground cumin	1 teaspoon ground coriander	1 teaspoon garam masala	juice of 1 lime	1 lb. 5 oz. boneless, skinless chicken breast, cubed

Combine 1 tablespoon of Ginger-garlic Paste (see page 26) with the ground spices and lime juice in a large mixing bowl. Add the chicken and season with salt. Stir well to coat the chicken with the mixture, rubbing the spices in with your fingers—if that doesn't put you off—then drizzle in 2 tablespoons of sunflower oil. Mix again, then cover and refrigerate for 1 hour or overnight if possible.

Preheat the oven to 400°F and line a baking sheet with foil.

Place the marinated chicken pieces on the prepared baking sheet in a single layer and bake in the oven for 15 minutes. Ensure the chicken is cooked right through by cutting open a piece and checking that it is completely white and hot inside.

Serve hot with a salad on the side.

BAIDA MALAI KADHI
Creamy Egg and Coconut Curry

In my cooking classes, people often ask me how long to boil an egg for to make a curry. I prefer the eggs to be well set so that they sit well in the sauce (see method below). Egg curries are popular in Indian homes, but are rarely found on restaurant menus. In India, eggs are considered non-vegetarian.

Serves 4

8 large free-range eggs	1 teaspoon ground turmeric	1 teaspoon Kashmiri chili powder	1 teaspoon garam masala	2 tablespoons tomato paste	1¾ cups coconut milk	a handful of fresh cilantro leaves, finely chopped, to garnish

Begin by hard-boiling the eggs. To do this, put the eggs in a single layer in a saucepan and then cover them with plenty of cold water. Bring to a boil, then reduce the heat so that the water simmers at a gentle bubble. Cook them for 12 minutes, then remove the pan from the heat and plunge the eggs into cold water to stop them cooking. Once they are cool, peel the eggs and cut them in half lengthwise. Set aside.

Heat 2 tablespoons of sunflower oil in a heavy-based saucepan and fry 1 tablespoon of Ginger-garlic Paste (see page 26) on high heat for a minute, stirring from time to time. Tip in the turmeric, chili powder, and garam masala and fry for a few seconds, then add 4 tablespoons of cold water. Reduce the heat to medium and cook until the water has evaporated, leaving the spices in oil.

Stir in the tomato paste and 2 tablespoons of cold water. Cook for 30 seconds, then pour in the coconut milk, season with salt, and heat through until almost boiling.

Place the eggs in the pan and baste them with the spice mixture.

Serve hot, sprinkled with the cilantro to garnish, along with some plain boiled rice to accompany.

BOMBAY TOAST
Herby Egg Toast

This is an easy Indian breakfast or light meal, and one that I often had growing up as a child in Bombay, as it was then called. We always ate this with ketchup! Serve it with baked beans or have it with a warming soup to make it heartier. Choose different breads for variation—I sometimes make this with slices of sourdough. Add extra chilies if you want more of a kick.

Serves 4

1 fresh green chili, finely chopped (seeds and all)	4 large free-range eggs, beaten	2 tablespoons finely chopped fresh cilantro leaves	8 slices of bread, white or brown	4 tablespoons grated hard cheese, such as Cheddar or Parmesan

Put the chili, ½ teaspoon of Ginger-garlic Paste (see page 26), eggs, cilantro, and some salt to taste in a large bowl and mix well.

Heat 1 tablespoon of sunflower oil in a large frying pan on high heat.

Dip the slices of bread into the egg mixture to coat, then shallow-fry, two slices of bread at a time, until they are golden on both sides and crispy at the edges, turning once, about 5–6 minutes.

Remove from the pan to a plate and cover with foil to keep hot while you cook the remaining slices in the same way, adding more sunflower oil to the pan and bringing it up to a high heat each time.

Serve hot, sprinkled with the cheese. Any leftover egg mixture can be scrambled and served as a topping.

BAIDA KHUMB ROLLS
Egg and Mushroom Rolls

A great dish for a light lunch, this omelet roll is a perfect combination of eggs and vegetables. Serve it with buttered bread—I love a seeded roll—and a green salad with cucumber and avocado. In India, this would be served with ketchup. I've used chestnut mushrooms here, but you could try any variety that you fancy. It is best to store eggs in the refrigerator as they will last longer.

Serves 4

8 large free-range eggs	1 teaspoon cumin seeds	1 lb. 1 oz. chestnut mushrooms, washed, patted dry and chopped	1 teaspoon ground turmeric	1 teaspoon Kashmiri chili powder	a small handful of fresh cilantro, finely chopped (stems and all)

Beat the eggs in a large bowl, season with salt, and set aside.

Warm 1 tablespoon of sunflower oil in a frying pan on high heat, add the cumin seeds and fry until they change color. Add 1 teaspoon of Ginger-garlic Paste (see page 26) and fry for 30 seconds.

Stir in the mushrooms and cook for about 5 minutes, or until softened, then add the turmeric and chili powder and cook until all the liquid has evaporated. Remove from the heat, tip into a bowl, set aside, and keep hot.

Wipe the pan with a paper towel and heat 1 tablespoon of sunflower oil on high heat, then pour in a quarter of the beaten eggs, allowing the mixture to evenly spread out over the base of the pan to make an omelet. When golden on the bottom, flip it over and cook the other side. Remove to a plate and keep warm while you make the remaining three omelets in the same way, adding a few drops of sunflower oil to the pan at the start of each one.

To serve, season the mushroom mixture with salt (adding salt before will make the mushroom mixture watery). Place one omelet on a serving plate and place a quarter of the mushroom mixture down the middle of it. Sprinkle with a little cilantro (reserving some for the garnish) and then fold in both the sides to make a roll. Do the same for the other three omelets. Sprinkle the remaining cilantro on top of the omelets and serve warm.

ANDE KI BHURJI
Spicy Scrambled Eggs

This simple dish takes minutes to prepare and makes a hearty breakfast or light lunch. I serve this with a buttered roll or with Rotis (see page 28). You can leave out the ham if you prefer—I sometimes swap this for cooked sausage, sliced mushrooms or mixed peppers. If using mushrooms or peppers, add them in after the tomatoes and cook until soft. Some cooks mix the raw chopped onions and tomatoes into the beaten eggs, but I prefer to cook them separately as this adds to the depth of flavor of the final dish.

Serves 4

8 large free-range eggs	1 teaspoon cumin seeds	1 large red onion, finely diced	2–3 fresh green or red chilies, finely chopped (seeds and all)	2 tomatoes, diced (seeds and all)	a good handful of fresh cilantro leaves, chopped	4 slices of good-quality ham, shredded

Beat the eggs in a large bowl, season with salt, and set aside.

Warm 2 tablespoons of sunflower oil in a frying pan on high heat, add the cumin seeds and fry until they darken and develop an aroma. Add the onion and fry for 3–4 minutes, until it begins to turn golden, then reduce the heat and cook on low heat for a further 2–3 minutes. Add the chilies and 1 teaspoon of Ginger-garlic Paste (see page 26) and fry for 30 seconds. Stir in the tomatoes and cook for 3–4 minutes, until soft, then stir in the cilantro.

Add the beaten eggs and cook on low heat, stirring all the time to scramble them. Take them off the heat when the eggs have nearly set and finish off the cooking by stirring the mixture—the pan will be hot enough to allow this. The eggs should be cooked but soft and glossy.

Mix in the shredded ham and serve hot with buttered rolls or Rotis (see page 28).

MASOORICHI AAMTI

Spiced Brown Lentils with Red Onion

Although I don't use red onion in many of my curries as I think they are often too sweet, here they go beautifully with the nutty, earthy flavors of brown lentils. A good way to shorten the cooking time for these lentils is to soak them in the morning, ready to cook them in the evening (or at night to use the next day, with a little forward planning!). To ensure that the lentils have cooked, either taste some or mash a few between your thumb and forefinger; they will keep their shape but should be completely soft.

Serves 4

1 cup brown lentils, washed and drained	1 large red onion, finely sliced	2 fresh green chilies, finely chopped (seeds and all)	1 teaspoon ground turmeric	1 teaspoon garam masala	2/3 cup coconut milk	2 tablespoons freshly chopped cilantro leaves, to garnish

Put the lentils into a large saucepan and add double the quantity of boiling water. Bring back to a boil, then cook on medium heat until they are mushy, about 45 minutes. Keep topping up the boiling water if the lentils become too dry; they must be submerged in water at all times. When done, the lentils will have broken down and thickened the cooking liquid.

Meanwhile, heat 2 tablespoons of sunflower oil in a separate, heavy-based saucepan and fry the onion on high heat until it begins to turn golden. Reduce the heat to medium and cook for a further 3–4 minutes, until very soft.

Stir in 2 teaspoons of Ginger-garlic Paste (see page 26) and the chilies and cook for a few seconds. Tip in the ground spices and cook until sizzling. Add a couple of tablespoons of cold water and cook on high heat until the water has evaporated.

Stir in the cooked lentils and the coconut milk, then season with salt and bring to a boil. Remove from the heat and sprinkle over the cilantro to garnish.

Serve hot with plain boiled rice or couscous.

MEEN PUTTU

Tuna Crumble with Chili and Cilantro

Although in Kerala in southern India this dish is made with fresh fish, such as
shark or kingfish, which is cooked and then flaked, I have recreated it here using
a can of tuna and a few other ingredients. This high-protein, hearty dish is a quick
midweek meal that I sometimes have on a baked potato, drizzled with lots of extra
virgin olive oil. You can swap the tuna for flaked salmon or tilapia, if you prefer.

Serves 4

☸	☸	☸	☸	☸	☸	☸
2 onions, finely diced	2 fresh green or red chilies, finely chopped (seeds and all)	8–10 fresh or 12 dried curry leaves, chopped or crumbled	1 teaspoon ground turmeric	a large handful of fresh cilantro leaves, finely chopped	4 x 5-ounce cans tuna in brine or spring water, drained	2 tablespoons fresh lemon or lime juice

Heat 2 tablespoons of sunflower oil in a large frying pan on high heat and fry
the onions for 3–4 minutes, then reduce the heat and cook them for a further
3–4 minutes, until very soft.

Add the chilies, curry leaves (standing back from the pan if using fresh leaves, as
they will splutter in the hot oil) and 2 teaspoons of Ginger-garlic Paste (see page 26)
and cook for 30 seconds.

Tip in the turmeric, cook for a minute, then add the cilantro and tuna. Add the
lemon or lime juice, season to taste with salt, and mix well. Cook for 2–3 minutes,
stirring from time to time, to heat the mixture through.

Serve hot, wrapped in Rotis (see page 28) with a few lettuce leaves, or spooned on
top of baked potatoes.

MIRCH MASALA AMALATE
Chili, Cheese, Cilantro, and Turmeric Omelet

A "masala amalate" or spiced omelet is eaten as breakfast, or sometimes as street food, where it makes a quick meal on the go. It is also considered a must-have at the much-loved Irani cafés of Mumbai—small restaurants that were set up by the Iranians who came to India a few hundred years ago. Have this with toast for a hearty, satisfying meal. You can personalize the heat level of this omelet by choosing one chili for less heat or two for a hotter one.

Serves 1

☗	☗	☗	☗	☗	☗	☗
1 small onion, finely chopped	1–2 fresh green chilies, finely chopped (seeds and all)	1 tomato, chopped (seeds and all)	2 large free-range eggs	½ teaspoon ground turmeric	1 tablespoon grated sharp Cheddar cheese	a handful of fresh cilantro leaves, finely chopped

Heat 1 tablespoon of sunflower oil in a frying pan, add the onion and fry on high heat for 2–3 minutes, until it begins to change color and turn golden. Reduce the heat and cook for a further 3–4 minutes, until soft.

Add the chilies and cook for a few seconds, then stir in the chopped tomato and cook for 2–3 minutes, until soft.

Meanwhile, beat the eggs in a bowl with the turmeric and some salt to taste.

Pour the beaten eggs into the pan and spread them out to evenly coat the onion mixture in the pan. Cover and cook on low heat until set to make an omelet. Sprinkle the cheese over the top and cook, covered, for a further minute.

Sprinkle over the cilantro, fold the omelet in half, and serve at once.

ANDE KA SALAAD

Egg Salad with Chili Mayonnaise

I love to serve this salad on a bed of crisp lettuce and some crunchy slices of cucumber as a summer lunch. It also makes a lovely side salad for a barbecue. You can swap the carrot for other crunchy vegetables, such as a celery stalk or a small zucchini, and sprinkle over a few raisins if you like a bit of sweetness.

Serves 4

½ teaspoon garam masala	3 tablespoons mayonnaise	1–2 fresh green chilies, finely chopped (seeds and all)	juice of ½ lime	a few fresh cilantro leaves, finely chopped	6 free-range eggs, hard-boiled (see page 55), peeled, and roughly chopped	2 small carrots, peeled and finely grated

Warm 1 teaspoon of sunflower oil in a small frying pan on high heat and add the garam masala. When it sizzles and develops an aroma, add a splash of cold water and cook on high heat until the water has evaporated. Remove from the heat and let cool.

In a serving bowl, combine the mayonnaise, cooled garam masala, the chilies, lime juice, cilantro, and some salt to taste. Add the eggs and carrots and toss gently to mix. Serve cold.

KHATTI MEETHI MACHLI
Sweet and Sour Salmon Bundles

This delicious recipe takes minutes to make and can be served with some seasonal vegetables on the side. You can buy tamarind pulp in the supermarket, but ensure you buy the chocolate-colored pulp or paste and not the dark, overly sour tamarind concentrate, which will change the look and taste of this dish. You can make your own tamarind pulp from "wet" tamarind (see page 12). Ensure that the marinade is quite smooth so that it coats the fish evenly.

Serves 4

☙	☙	☙	☙	☙	☙
1 teaspoon ground turmeric	1 teaspoon medium chili powder	3 tablespoons tamarind pulp (see page 12)	1 tablespoon soft brown cane sugar	4 x 7-ounce fillets of salmon, bream, or hake (skinless)	14 ounces new or baby potatoes, washed

Begin by making the marinade. Combine the ground turmeric, chili powder, tamarind pulp, and sugar in a small saucepan and season with salt. Cook on high heat until boiling and the sugar has dissolved, then remove from the heat and let cool completely.

Preheat the oven to 400°F.

Put the fish fillets into a bowl and rub the cold marinade over them using your fingers to coat them evenly. Leave for 20 minutes, or longer if you have the time.

When you are nearly ready to cook the fish, put the potatoes into a saucepan and cover with boiling water. Bring to a boil, then reduce the heat and simmer for 8–10 minutes, until you can easily put a knife through the largest one. Drain and halve.

Warm 1 tablespoon of sunflower oil in a frying pan and add the halved potatoes. Season with salt and a large pinch of black pepper and fry on high heat for 3–4 minutes, stirring from time to time, until they start to turn golden. Keep warm until the fish is cooked.

Meanwhile, put each marinated fish fillet on to a piece of foil, spoon over some of the marinade, and drizzle a little sunflower oil over the top of each one, then wrap each one to make an individual sealed bundle. Transfer the fish bundles to a baking sheet and bake in the oven for 15 minutes, or until cooked through.

Unwrap the fish and serve hot with the fried baby potatoes and a side salad.

FAST

MURGH MAKHANI
Easy Butter Chicken

This classic restaurant dish is so much tastier when made at home. However, it's worth bearing in mind that this is not meant to be a regular dish on the home menu—it's an occasional treat and perfect for entertaining.

The fenugreek leaves, available in Indian grocery stores, are essential to this dish, so don't leave them out. You could substitute the sweetened condensed milk for 3 tablespoons of honey and 4 tablespoons of light cream or coconut milk combined, if you wish. I use Kashmiri chili powder for this dish—it has a beautiful deep-red color without too much heat.

Serves 4

2 teaspoons medium-hot chili powder	2 teaspoons garam masala	1 lb. 5 oz. skinless chicken breasts, cubed	1 tablespoon butter	½ teaspoon kasoori methi (dried fenugreek leaves)	6 tablespoons tomato paste	4 tablespoons sweetened condensed milk

Preheat the oven to 400°F.

Sprinkle 1 teaspoon each of the chili powder and garam masala over the chicken pieces in a bowl. Add 1 tablespoon of Ginger-garlic Paste (see page 26) and season with salt. Mix well, then add 1 tablespoon of sunflower oil and mix again.

Transfer the chicken pieces to a baking sheet and spread them out in a single layer. Bake in the oven for 12–15 minutes, until white and hot all the way through when you cut a piece in half.

Meanwhile, make the sauce. Heat the butter and 1 tablespoon of sunflower oil in a saucepan until the butter is melted. Add 1 tablespoon of ginger-garlic paste and fry on high heat for 30 seconds, then add the kasoori methi and fry for a few seconds. Stir in the remaining chili powder and garam masala and fry for a few seconds. Pour in 4 tablespoons of cold water and bring to a boil. Cook on medium heat until the water has evaporated. Add the tomato paste and cook for 3–4 minutes, until blended, then pour in ⅔ cup of cold water. Bring to a boil, then reduce the heat and simmer for 2–3 minutes. The sauce should be of a thick, pouring consistency.

Mix the condensed milk with 7 tablespoons of warm water and add to the sauce. Season with salt, bring up to a boil, then fold in the hot cooked chicken.

Serve hot with Rotis (see page 28) or plain boiled rice and a side salad.

JHINGA SIMLA MIRCH

Shrimp and Green Peppers in a Tomato Curry

In north Indian cuisine, onions and tomatoes often form the base for curries. The red of ripe tomatoes and the blazing chili powder determine the color of the final dish. If the tomatoes you buy are pale and watery, you can add a tablespoon of tomato paste as well, to enhance the flavor. In this recipe, green peppers and shrimp make a lovely combination of fiber and protein, so that a carbohydrate in the form of rice or roti will make a complete, balanced meal.

Serves 4

2 onions, finely chopped	1 teaspoon ground turmeric	1 teaspoon Kashmiri chili powder	3 ripe red tomatoes, chopped (seeds and all)	2 large green peppers, cored, seeded, and diced	10½ ounces large fresh raw shrimp, shelled and deveined	a handful of fresh cilantro leaves, chopped, to garnish

Heat 2 tablespoons of sunflower oil in a frying pan and fry the onions on high heat for 3–4 minutes, until they begin to darken. Reduce the heat and cook for a further 3–4 minutes, until soft.

Stir in 2 teaspoons of Ginger-garlic Paste (see page 26) and cook for 30 seconds, then tip in the turmeric and chili powder and cook for another few seconds. Add 3–4 tablespoons of cold water to prevent the mixture from sticking to the pan and cook until the water has evaporated.

Stir in the tomatoes and cook for 3–4 minutes, until the mixture is soft and mushy. Add the green peppers, season with salt, and pour in a scant ½ cup of cold water to make a thick curry. Bring to a boil, then reduce the heat and cook, covered, for 8 minutes.

Stir in the shrimp and cook for a further 5 minutes, or until they turn pink.

Sprinkle over the cilantro to garnish, then serve hot with Rotis (see page 28) or plain boiled rice.

RAJMA PULAO
Red Bean and Coconut Rice

The sweetness of the onion and the coconut milk complements the saltiness of the rice, so ensure you season this dish well. You can use red onion if you want a sweeter flavor and add a couple of finely diced fresh green chilies along with the onion, if you'd like more heat. The rice gets a beautiful pink color from the red kidney beans that looks pretty served with a mixed green salad, such as lettuce and sliced avocado.

Serves 4

1 large onion, finely sliced	4 garlic cloves, finely chopped	1¼ cups basmati rice, washed and drained	½ x 14-ounce can red kidney beans, drained and rinsed	a big handful of fresh cilantro, finely chopped (stems and all)	scant 1 cup coconut milk mixed with the same amount of cold water

Heat 2 tablespoons of sunflower oil in a heavy-based saucepan and fry the onion and garlic on high heat for 3–4 minutes, then reduce the heat to medium and fry for a further 2 minutes, or until soft.

Add the rice and fry for 30 seconds, without stirring too much, then add the kidney beans, cilantro, and some salt and black pepper to taste.

Pour in the coconut milk and water mixture. Bring to a boil, then stir the rice once and cover. Reduce the heat to the lowest setting and simmer for 12 minutes without lifting the lid.

Remove from the heat and leave the pan, covered, for a further 5 minutes to allow the rice to finish cooking in the steam.

Remove the lid, fluff up the rice with a fork, and serve hot.

MASALA SAUSAGES
Spiced Sausages with Sweet Onion, Chili, and Cilantro

I sometimes use flavored sausages in this dish—my favorites are caramelized
onion or Cumberland. You can also use cooked sausages, which will make this dish
even quicker to prepare. I sometimes serve this dish with creamy mashed potatoes
and green vegetables, such as broccoli or green beans, on the side. You could also
serve it with rotis or pita breads.

Serves 4

2 red onions, diced	1 teaspoon medium-hot chili powder	1 teaspoon ground turmeric	1 red or yellow pepper, seeded, cored, and finely diced	2 tablespoons tomato paste	8 large pork or chicken sausages	a handful of fresh cilantro leaves, chopped, to garnish

Heat 2 tablespoons of sunflower oil in a frying pan and cook the onions on high heat
for 3–4 minutes, until they start to change color, then reduce the heat and cook for a
further 3–4 minutes, until soft.

Add 2 teaspoons of Ginger-garlic Paste (see page 26) and cook for 1 minute, then
add the chili powder and turmeric and cook for a few seconds.

Mix in the red or yellow pepper and fry on high heat for 4–5 minutes, until it begins
to soften, then reduce the heat, cover, and cook for a further 3–4 minutes. Tip in the
tomato paste, season with salt, and cook for a minute.

Meanwhile, heat a separate frying pan until hot, then fry the sausages, turning
regularly, for 10–15 minutes until cooked all the way through. Drain on paper towels,
then cut the sausages into ½-inch pieces and add to the onion pan. Mix well.

Garnish with the cilantro and serve with Rotis (see page 28) or pita breads.

MACCHI KI TIKKI
Quick Spiced Tuna Fishcakes

I serve these delicious fishcakes with a salad in the summer and steamed vegetables in the winter. When I'm organized and remember to plan ahead, I combine the mix of fish, chilies, lime juice, bread, and herbs in the morning before I begin work. In the evening, all I have to do is season with salt, shape the patties, dust with flour, and shallow-fry. Quick and easy! The lime juice takes away the fishy smell, making these fishcakes fragrant and delicious.

Makes 8 fishcakes

☸	☸	☸	☸	☸	☸	☸
2 slices of white bread	2 x 4-ounce cans tuna in brine, well drained	juice of 1 lime	1–2 fresh green chilies, finely chopped (seeds and all)	a small handful of fresh cilantro leaves, finely chopped	a few sprigs of dill, finely chopped	2 tablespoons all-purpose flour

Put the bread slices in a shallow dish, cover with cold water, and let soak for 5 minutes, then squeeze out to remove all the water.

Squeeze out any remaining brine from the tuna, then combine the tuna with the lime juice in a mixing bowl. Add the chilies and season with salt. Crumble the bread into the bowl, then mix in the cilantro and dill. Let stand for 10 minutes.

Divide and shape the tuna mixture into eight equal-size balls and then flatten each one to make a round patty/fishcake.

Heat enough sunflower oil to cover the base of a large frying pan on high heat. Dip each fishcake in the flour to coat, shaking off the excess, then shallow-fry for 4–5 minutes on each side, until golden brown, turning once.

Remove from the pan and drain on paper towels. Serve warm.

TAWA KOLAMBI
Bombay Fried Shrimp with Chili and Garlic

To butterfly fresh shelled shrimp, run a sharp knife down the outer curve of each shrimp's back and cut through until you can see the dark digestive tract. Lift this out and discard. Sometimes, it's colorless and at times there's none at all, but it's still worth butterflying shrimp as it makes them open out and appear larger, and also makes them more succulent. You can use rice flour or semolina to create a crust—rice flour gives a finer crust than semolina. These shrimp are a great family favorite in my home and they are so quick and easy to prepare.

Serves 4

1 teaspoon medium-hot chili powder	3 garlic cloves, grated or finely crushed	4 tablespoons rice flour or fine semolina	1 lb. 5 oz. large fresh raw shrimp, shelled, deveined, and butterflied (see above)	2 tablespoons fresh lime juice

Begin by making the marinade. Combine the chili powder, garlic, and a pinch of salt to taste in a bowl and then toss the shrimp in the marinade until coated. If you have the time, cover and leave this mixture in the refrigerator overnight, or for as long as you can.

Roll the marinated shrimp, a few at a time, in the rice flour or semolina until coated, then shake off any excess.

Heat enough sunflower oil in a large frying pan to lightly coat the base of the pan. Fry the shrimp (in batches) in the hot oil on high heat for 2–3 minutes on each side, until crisp and golden. Remove from the pan, drain on paper towels, and keep hot in foil while you cook the remaining shrimp in the same way.

Serve hot, drizzled with the lime juice.

KHEEMA MUTTAR
Spiced Ground Lamb with Peas

This is such a versatile recipe and a much-loved one in Indian homes. It can be served with rice and some plain yogurt, or wrapped in a roti, served on a baked potato or cooked in a sheet of puff pastry. You can swap the ground lamb for beef, if you prefer, and the peas can be swapped for sweet corn, diced mixed peppers, or sliced mushrooms. You can also finish it with a sprinkling of chopped fresh cilantro leaves, if you wish.

Serves 4

1 large onion, finely chopped	2 fresh green chilies, finely chopped (seeds and all)	2 tablespoons tomato paste	1 lb. 5 oz. boneless lamb, ground	¾ cup frozen garden peas	1 teaspoon ground turmeric	2 teaspoons garam masala

Warm 2 tablespoons of sunflower oil in a heavy-based saucepan. Add the onion and fry on high heat until it starts to change color, then reduce the heat and fry for a further 4–5 minutes until soft.

Add 2 teaspoons of Ginger-garlic Paste (see page 26) and the chilies and fry for 1 minute. Stir in the tomato paste, then cook until the oil separates, adding a few tablespoons of cold water to prevent the mixture from sticking.

Add the ground lamb, breaking it up with a wooden spoon as you go until it is all loose and separate. Keep cooking on high heat, stirring regularly, until the lamb has all turned from pink to brown.

Add the peas, turmeric, garam masala, and some salt to taste and mix well. Cover, reduce the heat to low, and cook until the lamb is done, about 10 minutes. Serve hot.

LOBHIA AUR GUCCHI KI SUBZI
Black-eyed peas with Mushrooms

The aroma of cumin in this dish is what makes it special, but make sure you cook the seeds carefully—put them into oil that's just warm and then wait for them to sizzle, change color, and develop an aroma. All this takes no time at all. The color should be a golden brown—if they get too dark, it's a sign that they're burnt! Black-eyed peas are an Indian home staple—they are high in soluble fiber, which helps the body to eliminate cholesterol, and they are filling and delicious, too!

Serves 4

1 teaspoon cumin seeds	1 teaspoon medium-hot chili powder	1 teaspoon ground turmeric	1 teaspoon garam masala	3 tomatoes, finely diced (seeds and all)	14-ounce can black-eyed peas, drained and rinsed	10½ ounces closed cup mushrooms, washed, patted dry, and thickly sliced

Warm 1 tablespoon of sunflower oil in a frying pan, then add the cumin seeds and fry on high heat for 30 seconds or until they start to darken. Add 2 teaspoons of Ginger-garlic Paste (see page 26) and fry for 30 seconds. Add the chili powder, turmeric, and garam masala, fry for a few seconds, then pour in a couple of tablespoons of cold water. Cook until the water has evaporated and the oil separates.

Tip in the tomatoes and cook on high heat for 4–5 minutes, until they are soft. Stir in the black-eyed peas, mushrooms, and some salt to taste. Cover and bring to a boil, then reduce the heat and simmer for 3–4 minutes. Remove from the heat and mash a few peas, if necessary, to add thickness to the sauce.

Serve hot with plain boiled rice or couscous.

MURGH MASALA
Family-style Chicken Curry

I've used boneless chicken here as it cooks quite quickly—you can use legs or thighs on the bone, if you prefer, but ensure you increase the cooking time at the end to 30 minutes, or until the chicken, when cut open, is white and hot all the way through. When cooking chicken, ensure you put it into a hot pan and leave it to shrink a bit before flipping the pieces. If it is moved too soon, the flesh may shred and stick to the pan. A home-style curry typically has a wetter sauce than a restaurant-style curry.

Serves 4

1 teaspoon ground turmeric	1 teaspoon Kashmiri chili powder	1 teaspoon garam masala	1 lb. 5 oz. boneless, skinless chicken breasts/ thighs, cubed	2 onions, finely sliced	2 tablespoons tomato paste	a few sprigs of fresh cilantro, chopped

Combine the turmeric, chili powder, garam masala, and some salt with the chicken in a bowl, mix well and then stir in a teaspoon of sunflower oil to seal the spices to the chicken. Cover and let marinate in the refrigerator while you make the sauce.

Heat 1 tablespoon of sunflower oil in a heavy-based saucepan and add the onions, then cook on high heat for 3–4 minutes until they begin to change color. Reduce the heat and continue to cook for a further 4–5 minutes, until they are very soft. Add a tablespoon of Ginger-garlic Paste (see page 26), fry for 30 seconds, then stir in the tomato paste and fry for a minute.

Add a small handful of the cilantro, reserving some for the garnish. Remove from the heat, carefully transfer the mixture to a blender, add enough cold water to just cover the mixture, then blend to a fine puree. Set aside.

Heat 2 tablespoons of sunflower oil in the same pan on high heat, then add the marinated chicken pieces and fry lightly to seal in the juices, for about 4 minutes. Add a couple of tablespoons of cold water and cook the chicken for a further minute.

Add the sauce from the blender to the chicken. Rinse the blender with a couple of tablespoons of cold water and add that to the pan as well. Bring to a boil, then reduce the heat to low. Cover and cook for 10–12 minutes, until the chicken is cooked through.

Sprinkle over the reserved cilantro, then serve with plain boiled rice or Rotis (see page 28) and salad.

VEGETABLE PATTIES
Vegetable Curry Puffs

The Irani Zoroastrian immigrants who came to India from around the 1800s set up cafés, or "chai khanas," and bakeries that provided these cafés with cookies, cakes, and pastries like this one. These are eaten with ketchup and washed down with tea, which you can ask for sweetened with condensed milk—customers joke that it is so thick that a spoon can stand upright in it!

Makes 8 curry puffs

1 onion, finely diced	3 small fresh green chilies, finely chopped (seeds and all)	1 tablespoon tomato paste	1 teaspoon ground turmeric	1 teaspoon garam masala	7 ounces mixed diced frozen vegetables (such as carrots, green beans, and peas)	1 x 11¼-ounce ready-rolled puff pastry sheet

Heat 2 tablespoons of sunflower oil in a frying pan and fry the onion on high heat for 4–5 minutes, until the color starts to change. Reduce the heat and cook for a further 3–4 minutes, until soft and a piece can be cut easily with the edge of a spoon.

Add 1 tablespoon of Ginger-garlic Paste (see page 26) and the chilies and fry for 30 seconds, then stir in the tomato paste and fry for 1–2 minutes, until blended. Add the ground spices, cook for a few seconds, then add a couple of tablespoons of cold water. Cook on high heat until the water has evaporated and the mixture thickened.

Add the frozen vegetables, then season with salt. Half-cover the vegetables with hot water, then bring to a boil. Reduce the heat, cover, and cook for 25–30 minutes, until the vegetables are very soft. Roughly mash with a potato masher.

Preheat the oven to 400°F.

Lay the sheet of pastry on a lightly floured surface and cut into eight rectangles. Spoon some of the vegetable mix on to one side of a rectangle and then fold the other side over to make a package. Press the edges together to completely seal, then press down around the edges with a fork. Repeat with the remaining rectangles.

Prick the surface of each package a couple of times with the fork so that steam can escape while the puffs cook. Transfer the packages to a baking sheet and bake for about 20 minutes, until golden brown. Serve hot.

MURGH MASALA ROLL
Spicy Chicken Wraps

I've used cooked chicken in this recipe—you can either buy this, use leftover cooked chicken, or cook a couple of chicken breasts, either in the oven or poached in enough water to cover them, with a bit of salt. This can be done in advance and the cooked chicken frozen to save some time. If poaching, save the liquid and freeze that as well—it's a good base for soups and stews. I find that if I have cooked chicken breast in the freezer, lots of weeknight meals become simpler—even making a quick chicken soup takes just minutes! You can add some salad greens or sliced tomato and cucumber to the wraps if you want to.

Serves 4

4 tablespoons white wine vinegar	4 fresh green or red chilies, finely chopped (seeds and all)	2 onions, finely diced	1 teaspoon ground turmeric	1 teaspoon garam masala	14 ounces cooked skinless chicken breast, shredded or chopped into small pieces	4 wholewheat soft flour or corn wraps

Combine the vinegar and half of the chilies in a small glass bowl and set aside.

Heat 2 tablespoons of sunflower oil in a frying pan and fry the onions on high heat for 4–5 minutes, until the color starts to change. Reduce the heat and cook for a further 3–4 minutes, until soft.

Add 2 teaspoons of Ginger-garlic Paste (see page 26) and the remaining chilies and cook for 30 seconds. Stir in the ground spices and cook for a few seconds, then add a couple of tablespoons of cold water and cook on high heat until the water has evaporated. Stir in the cooked chicken pieces and season with salt.

Warm the wraps individually, on both sides, in a separate frying pan.

To assemble, place one of the wraps on a serving plate. Arrange some of the chicken mixture down the center. Drizzle with some of the chili and vinegar mixture, including a few chopped chilies. Fold the wrap upward from the bottom and then fold the sides inward, ensuring that they overlap, to make a roll.

Assemble the remaining wraps in a similar way, then serve.

HEARTY

MASHYACHI AMTI
Fish Curry with Coconut and Pepper

This dish is from the west coast of India, and it brings together local ingredients, such as coconut and tamarind, in a burst of salty, sour flavors. Great big tamarind trees bear sour, pulpy fruit in the summer. The fruit is shelled and the pods removed and rolled into balls or flattened into cakes to preserve them for use later on in the year. Mackerel is used for this curry in India, but you can also use fillets of any firm fish, such as hake or coley.

Serves 4

2 whole mackerel (heads removed), gutted, cleaned, and cut widthwise into thick steaks	2 teaspoons ground turmeric	1 teaspoon black peppercorns	6 dried Kashmiri red chilies, broken into bits	1 onion, sliced	4 tablespoons dried shredded coconut	3 tablespoons tamarind pulp (see page 12)

Rub the pieces of fish with half of the turmeric and enough salt to season. Set aside.

Warm 1 tablespoon of sunflower oil in a frying pan, then fry the peppercorns and dried chilies on high heat for 2–3 minutes, until an aroma develops. Tip in the onion and cook on high heat for 3–4 minutes, until it begins to change color, then reduce the heat and cook for a further 5 minutes, or until soft. Add the coconut and continue to fry until the coconut turns light brown.

Remove from the heat, carefully transfer the mixture into a blender, add enough cold water to cover the mixture, and blend until smooth. Set aside.

Wipe the pan with a paper towel and heat 2 tablespoons of sunflower oil in it, then fry 2 teaspoons of Ginger-garlic Paste (see page 26) on high heat for 1 minute. Stir in the tamarind pulp and bring up to a sizzle. Add the sauce from the blender, then rinse the blender with 3–4 tablespoons of cold water and add that to the pan as well. Bring to a boil and season with salt.

Slip the fish pieces into the curry, then cook on medium heat, covered, for around 8 minutes, or until the fish is cooked.

Serve hot with plain boiled rice.

PORK CURRY
Tangy Goan-style Pork Curry

Pork is not often seen on Indian menus due to religious restrictions. However, the Christian communities of India in places like Goa, Mangalore, and Kerala cook wonderful pork dishes using local spices. I have used pork loin fillet, but you can also use pork loin steaks, trimmed of the fat. The Kashmiri chilies give this dish its unique rich red color, which is complemented by the brown malt vinegar. I sometimes like to add a dash of balsamic vinegar to enrich the color and taste of this dish.

Serves 4

10 dried red Kashmiri chilies, seeded	1 lb. 5 oz. pork loin fillet, cubed	1 teaspoon ground turmeric	1 large onion, sliced	1 tablespoon garam masala	5 tablespoons brown malt vinegar

Put the dried chilies in a heatproof bowl, cover with a scant ½ cup of boiling water and let soak for 10 minutes.

Mix the pork, turmeric, and some salt to season in a large mixing bowl, then set aside while you prepare the curry paste.

Blend the onion, 2 teaspoons of Ginger-garlic Paste (see page 26), soaked chilies (along with the soaking liquid), garam masala, and vinegar in a blender until very finely chopped and combined.

Heat 2 tablespoons of sunflower oil in a heavy-based saucepan and fry the pork on high heat until well sealed all over, about 3–4 minutes, stirring regularly to prevent it from sticking. Add a few teaspoons of cold water if the meat starts to stick.

Add the curry paste and stir to blend, then season with salt. Pour in enough boiling water (scant 1 cup) to make a pouring consistency and then bring to a boil. Reduce the heat, cover, and cook gently for about 1 hour, or until the pork is tender.

Serve hot with Rotis (see page 28) and a side salad.

SAAS NI MACCHI

Parsi-style White Fish Curry with Vinegar

This fish in white sauce is a festive dish served at Parsi weddings, and traditionally the fish used is silver pomfret, which is mild and delicate in taste. I've taken the liberty of using cod as pomfret is not easily available in the West. There are many versions of this curry—I have eaten this sweet and sometimes not, with the addition of mint, eggs, or tomatoes, and sometimes without. This recipe is how I like it—it tastes best when it's a mix of salty, tangy, and sweet. Traditional cooks would use a brown sugar cane vinegar called Parsi vinegar, but I've used brown malt vinegar here.

Serves 4

⚜	⚜	⚜	⚜	⚜	⚜	⚜
1 teaspoon cumin seeds	2 fresh green chilies, minced (seeds and all)	7–8 fresh curry leaves, chopped, or a large pinch of dried curry leaves, crumbled	3 teaspoons all-purpose flour	2 teaspoons white sugar	2 tablespoons brown malt vinegar	2 large cod fillets, skinned and cut into 4 pieces, each about 2½ inches long and 1½ inches wide

Put 1¾ cups of cold water in a measuring cup and set aside.

Warm 2 tablespoons of sunflower oil in a frying pan on high heat, then add the cumin seeds. When they sizzle and darken, reduce the heat and add the chilies, curry leaves, and 1 teaspoon of Ginger-garlic Paste (page 26). Cook for 30 seconds and then stir in the flour. Cook on medium heat for 1 minute, stirring constantly, then reduce the heat and cook for a further minute, again stirring until it develops a cooked aroma but no color.

Pour in half of the measured cold water and whisk to remove any lumps of flour. When the mixture is fairly smooth, add the remaining water and cook on high heat, whisking to blend. Season with salt, add the sugar and vinegar, and bring to a boil, stirring frequently to prevent lumps forming. Reduce the heat and simmer for 3–4 minutes, until the sauce has thickened a bit.

Now slip the fish pieces in gently and cook on medium heat for 7–8 minutes, or until the fish is tender.

Serve hot with plain boiled rice.

MALAIWALA GOSHT
Creamy Lamb Curry

Awadh was the ancient name for Lucknow in northern India. The distinct cuisine here, called "Awadhi," was created for the ruling Nawabs of royal India and is known for its delicate flavors and slow cooking. Here is an updated version of an old royal recipe. I often serve this at dinner parties, with some soft rotis and a side salad.

Serves 4

1 lb. 5 oz. lean, boneless lamb, trimmed and cubed	2 onions, sliced	3 fresh green chilies, roughly chopped (seeds and all)	1 tablespoon tomato paste	2 tablespoons garam masala	1 cup Greek yogurt	scant ½ cup heavy cream

Heat 3 tablespoons of sunflower oil in a heavy-based saucepan and fry the lamb on high heat until well sealed all over, about 3–4 minutes. Stir frequently so that the meat does not stick to the pan.

Tip in the onions and fry, stirring from time to time, until they turn golden. Stir in 2 tablespoons of Ginger-garlic Paste (see page 26), the chilies, tomato paste, and garam masala and give everything a good stir. Fry for 2–3 minutes, then add 2 cups of boiling water and bring to a boil.

Pour in the yogurt and season with salt. Cover and cook on high heat to bring the curry back to a boil, then reduce the heat to low and cook for about an hour, until the meat is tender. Check the curry from time to time and add a little more boiling water if it gets too dry. There should be a sauce of pouring consistency in the pan.

Lift the meat out of the curry with a slotted spoon and set aside. Strain the curry sauce through a strainer into a bowl and discard the contents of the strainer.

Return the strained curry sauce to the pan, stir in the cream and adjust the seasoning to taste. Return the meat to the curry, then heat through gently.

Serve hot with plain boiled rice or Rotis (see page 28) and a crunchy green salad.

PALAK MURGH
Chicken and Spinach Curry

We have an unwritten rule at my home that a weeknight meal has to be ready to eat in about 45 minutes. I often make this dish, with rice on the side, so that the three food groups—protein, fiber, and carbohydrates—are included. You can, if you wish, wilt the spinach by cooking it with a couple of tablespoons of cold water in a saucepan and then whizzing it in a blender. I've used it chopped up here, for added texture. Always wash bags of unwashed fresh spinach thoroughly—there is nothing worse than finding grit in a spinach curry!

Serves 4

2 large onions, finely diced	2 tablespoons tomato paste	1 lb. 5 oz boneless chicken breasts or thighs, skinned and cubed	1 teaspoon ground turmeric	1 teaspoon medium-hot chili powder	1 teaspoon garam masala	7 ounces fresh spinach, washed and chopped

Heat 2 tablespoons of sunflower oil in a frying pan and fry the onions on high heat for 4–5 minutes, until they start to change color. Reduce the heat and cook for a further 3–4 minutes, until they are soft and can be cut easily with the edge of a spoon.

Add 2 tablespoons of Ginger-garlic Paste (see page 26) and fry for 30 seconds, then add the tomato paste and fry for a couple of minutes.

Add the chicken pieces and fry on high heat to seal in the juices, then add the ground spices. Season with salt, pour in about ⅔ cup of cold water, and bring to a boil. Reduce the heat, cover, and cook for 10 minutes, or until the chicken is tender and is white and hot all the way through when a piece is cut open.

Stir in the spinach and bring to a boil again. Adjust the seasoning to taste. Serve hot with Rotis (see page 28) or plain boiled rice.

CHILLI PANEER
Indo-Chinese-style Spicy Paneer with Onion and Green Pepper

Indo-Chinese cooking is second in popularity to Indian food in India. It is a spicy, intensely flavored, hybrid cuisine that has signature dishes combining Chinese cooking techniques and ingredients such as soy sauce with Indian ones such as chilies and paneer. It was possibly created by a tiny Chinese community that migrated to India around 100 years ago. Today, it is as popular as street food where noodles are tossed with spices for a quick meal, or at fine dining restaurants where celebrity chefs create culinary masterpieces.

Serves 4

3 tablespoons tomato ketchup	2 tablespoons hot red chili sauce	4 teaspoons dark soy sauce	1 tablespoon brown malt vinegar	9 ounces paneer, cut into ½-inch cubes	1 large onion, cut into large squares	1 large green pepper, cored, seeded, and cubed

Preheat the oven to 400°F.

Mix the ketchup, chili sauce, soy sauce, and vinegar in a bowl and set aside.

Put the paneer in a large mixing bowl, season with some salt and drizzle in a few drops of sunflower oil. Mix well. Transfer the paneer pieces to a baking sheet and spread them out in a single layer. Bake in the oven for 12–15 minutes, until golden.

Heat 2 tablespoons of sunflower oil in a large frying pan, then cook 2 tablespoons of Ginger-garlic Paste (see page 26) on medium heat for 30 seconds. Increase the heat to high, add the onion and green pepper, and cook for 3–4 minutes, stirring, until the vegetables start to soften but still retain their crunch.

Stir in the ketchup mixture and cook for 3–4 minutes, then season with salt, bearing in mind that soy sauce is salty. Fold in the baked paneer.

Serve hot on its own or with plain boiled rice or noodles, if you like.

CHANNE AUR ANAAR KA SALAAD
Hearty Chickpea and Pomegranate Salad

My grandmother taught me to prepare a pomegranate by cutting it in half, then into quarters and scooping the seeds out gently with my fingers. This meant that there wasn't too much splashing of juice and the process was fairly easy and quick. I find doing this very therapeutic even today, but if you can't be bothered with it all, you can buy prepared pomegranate seeds at most grocery stores. These are much more expensive than buying the whole fruit though.

Serves 4

1 teaspoon cumin seeds	14-ounce can chickpeas, drained and rinsed	5 tablespoons finely diced, cored and seeded mixed peppers	3 tablespoons pomegranate seeds	generous pinch of white caster sugar	dash of fresh lemon juice	2 teaspoons finely chopped fresh cilantro leaves

Warm a small frying pan on high heat and add the cumin seeds (keep a mortar and pestle or a spice mill close by). As soon as the pan gets hot, in a matter of seconds, they will darken and develop an aroma. Remove from the heat and tip the cumin seeds into the mortar or spice mill, then crush them to a fine powder.

In a serving bowl, combine the chickpeas with all the remaining ingredients, plus the toasted cumin powder, 2 teaspoons of sunflower oil, and some salt to taste. Serve at room temperature.

TIP

If you are making this salad in advance, combine the sunflower oil, salt, sugar, and lemon juice in a small jar, then combine the remaining ingredients, including the toasted cumin powder, in a separate bowl. Cover and store both in the refrigerator. Just before serving, shake the bottle well and drizzle the dressing over the salad.

KALI DAL
Black Lentils with Garlic and Chili

Black beans or lentils are called "urad beans" or "urid beans." They have a unique creamy texture when cooked which is unlike other beans and lentils. Soaking them overnight reduces the cooking time, but slow, long cooking is what gives them a creamy, soft texture. This dal is time-consuming to make but tastes absolutely delicious. It's a good idea to make a batch and freeze some. Some cooks combine it with lentils, such as urid dal, which is actually the split, skinned black beans themselves. This gives the final dish a buttery finish. Most Indian cooks cook black urad beans in a pressure cooker to reduce the cooking time.

Serves 4

scant 1 cup black lentils (urad beans)	1 teaspoon ground turmeric	1 teaspoon medium chili powder	1 teaspoon garam masala	6 garlic cloves, finely chopped	2 tablespoons chopped fresh cilantro leaves	juice of 1 lemon

Put the black lentils in a large bowl, cover with plenty of boiling water, and let soak overnight.

The next day, drain the lentils and rinse in a strainer under cold water. Put the lentils in a heavy-based saucepan, along with the ground spices, and then pour in enough boiling water to cover them, about 1¼ cups. Bring to a boil, then reduce the heat and simmer for an hour or a bit longer, until the lentils can be easily mashed between your forefinger and thumb. You will need to keep topping up the boiling water as the lentils cook and absorb the liquid (you can add boiling water, or add cold water and then return to a boil each time, if you prefer).

Heat 2 tablespoons of sunflower oil in a separate small, heavy-based saucepan and fry the garlic for 3–4 minutes, until it turns golden. Pour this into the cooked lentils, season with salt and then stir in the cilantro, followed by the lemon juice.

Serve hot with plain boiled rice or Rotis (see page 28).

PANEER FRIED RICE
Indo-Chinese-style Rice with Spiced Paneer

This has to be one of my favorite things to eat after a long working day. If I know I'll be home late, I prepare some of the ingredients in the morning before I leave home—I chop the onions, make the sauce mixture, and cook the paneer, so that at the end of the day, there's very little to do before we can eat. You can add more vegetables to this—try diced carrots and green beans—they'll go into the pan with the onions and take about 7–8 minutes to cook.

Serves 4

9 ounces paneer, cubed	1¼ cups basmati rice, washed and drained	3 tablespoons tomato ketchup	4 teaspoons dark soy sauce	4 fresh green chilies, finely diced (seeds and all)	2 onions, cut into large pieces	3 scallions, both white and green parts chopped

Preheat the oven to 400°F. Line a baking sheet with foil.

Season the paneer with salt in a bowl and mix well. Drizzle in 1 tablespoon of sunflower oil and mix again. Spread the paneer out on the lined baking sheet in a single layer, then bake in the oven for 15 minutes, turning over halfway through the cooking time.

Meanwhile, put the rice into a deep saucepan, add three times the volume of boiling water and bring to a boil. Reduce the heat and simmer for 10 minutes, or until cooked, then drain through a colander. Set aside and keep hot.

Mix the ketchup and soy sauce in a bowl and set aside.

Heat 1 tablespoon of sunflower oil in a frying pan, add 2 tablespoons of Ginger-garlic Paste (see page 26) and the chilies and cook on high heat for 30 seconds, or until an aroma develops. Add the onions and cook for 3–4 minutes, or until they start to soften. Season with salt, then stir in the ketchup mixture. Cook for a minute or so on high heat until the mixture comes to a boil. The onions should still have a bit of crunch.

Fold in the paneer, then sprinkle in the scallions and heat through until hot. Fold in the drained rice and serve hot.

KHEEME KA PIE
Indian-style Shepherd's Pie

We often have this warming dish in the winter, and sometimes I add a big splash of balsamic vinegar or Worcestershire sauce to the ground meat as it cooks. It's also good for entertaining as it can be made in advance and heated just before serving. You can spice up the mashed potatoes by adding a couple of finely diced fresh green chilies, then scattering some grated Cheddar cheese on top before baking.

Serves 4

3 large potatoes	1 large onion, finely chopped	2 fresh green chilies, finely chopped (seeds and all)	1 lb. 2 oz. ground lamb or beef	2 teaspoons garam masala	14-ounce can chopped tomatoes

Put the potatoes, unpeeled, in a large saucepan with enough boiling water to cover them. Bring to a boil, then reduce the heat, cover, and simmer for 35–40 minutes, until you can put a knife through the center of each one. Drain them in a strainer and refresh under running cold water, then set aside to cool.

Meanwhile, warm 2 tablespoons of sunflower oil in a heavy-based saucepan. Add the onion and fry on high heat until it starts to change color, then reduce the heat and fry until soft, about 4–5 minutes. Add 2 teaspoons of Ginger-garlic Paste (see page 26) and the chilies and fry for a minute.

Add the ground lamb or beef, breaking it up with a wooden spoon as you go, and cook on high heat, stirring frequently, until it is well browned. Add the garam masala, season with salt, and mix well. Pour in the tomatoes and cook for 3–4 minutes, then cover, reduce the heat to low, and simmer until the meat is cooked, about 15 minutes.

Preheat the oven to 400°F.

Peel the cooled potatoes and mash them with a potato masher or ricer until smooth. Season with salt and fold in 1 tablespoon of sunflower oil.

Transfer the ground meat mixture to a baking dish and top it with the mashed potato, covering the meat mixture completely. Bake in the oven for 30–35 minutes, until slightly brown on top. Serve hot.

CHANNE KA SHORBA
Chickpea and Chorizo Stew

This satisfying stew is so easy to prepare as it contains mostly pantry ingredients. You can use canned chopped tomatoes if you want more texture, but I like to use passata, which is a thick puree of strained tomatoes, so that you don't get any skin or seeds. You can substitute the chickpeas with red kidney beans or lima beans for variety, or even use a can of mixed beans. I always rinse the beans in a strainer to get rid of the salt and sludge that collects at the bottom of the can.

Serves 4

1 teaspoon cumin seeds	2 cups strained tomatoes	14-ounce can chickpeas, drained and rinsed	a pinch of freshly ground black pepper	a small handful of fresh cilantro leaves, finely chopped	4½ ounces paneer, diced into bite-size pieces	2¼ ounces chorizo, thickly sliced

Warm 1 tablespoon of sunflower oil in a heavy-based saucepan on high heat and fry the cumin seeds for a few seconds, until they begin to turn dark. Add 1 teaspoon of Ginger-garlic Paste (see page 26) and cook for a minute or so, stirring.

Tip in the strained tomatoes and the chickpeas. Season with salt (bearing in mind that the chorizo is quite salty) and black pepper and pour in scant 1 cup boiling water. Bring to a boil, then reduce the heat and simmer for a few minutes to blend the flavors.

Stir in the cilantro, paneer, and chorizo and cook on high heat for 3–4 minutes, until the paneer and chorizo soften. Serve hot.

TIP
If you are preparing this in advance, add the last three ingredients when you reheat the stew just before serving.

ONE POT

MURGH KAJU KA SHORBA
Spiced Chicken Soup with Cashews and Coconut

I sometimes add a bit of pasta to make this soup heartier, or serve it with a crusty baguette, liberally buttered. You could use other nuts, such as almonds, or if you don't want to use nuts at all, substitute the cashews with 2 tablespoons of sunflower seeds, or add a finely diced raw potato to add body to the soup.

Serves 4

10½ ounces skinless chicken breasts, left whole	2 bay leaves	2 large carrots, peeled and finely diced	2 tablespoons cashews	scant 1 cup coconut milk

Heat 1 tablespoon of sunflower oil in a saucepan and fry 1 tablespoon of Ginger-garlic Paste (see page 26) on high heat for 30 seconds, until it sizzles and the raw garlic smell disappears.

Add the chicken breasts, bay leaves, carrots, and cashews, along with 1¾ cups of cold water, and bring to a boil. Reduce the heat and simmer for about 30 minutes, or until the chicken is white and hot all the way through when a breast is cut through the center with a knife.

Lift the chicken breasts and bay leaves out with a slotted spoon. Discard the bay leaves and chop the chicken into bite-size pieces.

Cool the mixture slightly, then transfer it to a blender and blend until smooth.

Pour the sauce from the blender into the same pan and add the coconut milk. Season with salt and black pepper and heat through until hot.

Put the cooked chicken pieces into the bottom of four soup bowls and then pour in the soup. Serve very hot.

KOZHI ISHTU
South Indian Chicken and Potato Stew

South Indian cooking is known for its use of aromatic spices, such as black pepper. In Kerala, chicken stew is a breakfast dish that is traditionally served with "appams" or hoppers—lacy pancakes made with rice and coconut—and is often eaten on Christmas Day. If you like, you can add carrots and peas for more fiber, or throw in two or three fresh green chilies along with the onions for a bit of heat. I prefer the lovely fragrance of black pepper that shines through, making this a simple yet delicious meal.

Serves 4

1 onion, chopped	1 teaspoon ground turmeric	10 fresh curry leaves or 15 dried ones, chopped or crumbled	1 large potato, peeled and finely chopped	10½ ounces skinless chicken breasts, chopped into small pieces	1 teaspoon freshly crushed black pepper	1¾ cups coconut milk

Heat 2 tablespoons of sunflower oil in a saucepan, add the onion, and fry on high heat for about 3–4 minutes, stirring from time to time, until it starts to soften.

Add 2 teaspoons of Ginger-garlic Paste (see page 26) and cook for a minute. Add the turmeric and cook for a further minute, then stir in the curry leaves. Tip in the potato and cook for 3–4 minutes, stirring occasionally, until the potato pieces start to turn translucent.

Now add the chicken pieces, season with some salt and the black pepper and mix well. Cook the chicken on high heat until it is sealed all over and looks white not pink on the surface.

Pour in scant 1 cup of boiling water. Bring to a boil, then reduce the heat, cover, and simmer until the chicken and potato pieces are almost cooked, about 12–13 minutes.

Pour in the coconut milk, bring back to a boil, then reduce the heat and simmer for 2–3 minutes, until the chicken and potatoes are tender—you should be able to easily cut through a piece of potato, and the chicken should be white and hot all the way through when you cut a piece in half.

Serve hot, with Rotis (see page 28).

GUCCHI TAMATAR KA PULAO
Mushroom, Carrot, and Tomato Rice

This easy recipe needs nothing except a salad or some plain yogurt on the side to make it a more satisfying meal. Oyster, shiitake, and chestnut mushrooms give it a rich, intense flavor, so if you want a milder-tasting dish, it's best to use closed cup white mushrooms. Clean the mushrooms thoroughly by washing them and patting them dry with a dish towel. Although some recipes say that mushrooms should just be wiped as they can absorb water during washing, here, they are cooked in liquid so washing them won't matter. When cooking rice, don't stir it too much as this can break the grains and make the rice stodgy.

Serves 4

1 onion, finely chopped	6 garlic cloves, finely chopped	1 teaspoon medium chili powder	3 teaspoons tomato paste	1 carrot, peeled and coarsely grated	3½ ounces mixed mushrooms (such as oyster, shiitake, chestnut or closed cup white mushrooms), washed, patted dry and sliced	1¼ cups basmati rice, washed and drained

Heat 2 tablespoons of sunflower oil in a heavy-based saucepan and fry the onion on high heat for 3–4 minutes, until it starts to turn golden. Add the garlic, reduce the heat to medium, and fry for a further 3–4 minutes.

Add the chili powder and cook for a few seconds, then stir in the tomato paste. Mix in the carrot and mushrooms, then tip in the rice and mix well.

Pour in 1¾ cups boiling water and season with salt. Stir once gently and bring to a boil, then reduce the heat, cover with a tight-fitting lid, and simmer for 12 minutes, without lifting the lid. Turn off the heat and leave the pan covered for a further 5 minutes to finish cooking the rice in the steam.

Remove the lid, fluff up the rice with a fork, and serve hot.

KHUBANI KA GOSHT
Lamb and Apricot Curry

This recipe is inspired by the Parsi cooking of India—the Parsis came to India many centuries ago from Persia, and brought with them a cuisine that is delicious and unique. The combination of meat and fruit is not usually found in Indian cooking—in many such dishes, there is an influence of Mughal or Parsi cuisine. In this recipe, you can use dried apricots found in the West or try Hunza apricots found in many Indian stores. These are denser, drier, and sweeter than the orange ones and need to be pitted before use.

Serves 4

1 cup dried apricots, pitted	1 lb. 5 oz. lean, boneless lamb, trimmed and cubed	1 teaspoon medium chili powder	1 teaspoon ground turmeric	2 teaspoons garam masala	2 large onions, finely sliced	1 cup Greek yogurt

Put the dried apricots in a heatproof bowl, cover with boiling water and let soak for 15 minutes, then drain off any excess liquid. Set aside.

Mix the lamb with the ground spices and some salt in a bowl. Cover and set aside while you make the curry sauce.

Heat 1½ tablespoons of sunflower oil in a heavy-based saucepan and add the onions. Fry on high heat for 4–5 minutes, until they start to turn brown, then reduce the heat and cook for a further 4–5 minutes, until soft and golden brown in color. Add 2 teaspoons of Ginger-garlic Paste (see page 26) and cook for a further minute.

Remove from the heat, carefully transfer the mixture to a blender, along add cold water to barely cover the mixture, then blend to a fine puree.

Heat 1½ tablespoons of sunflower oil in the same pan and fry the lamb on high heat until it is well sealed all over. Pour in 3–4 tablespoons of cold water and bring to a boil. Stir in the yogurt and cook for 3–4 minutes, then add the sauce from the blender. Rinse the blender with a couple of tablespoons of cold water and add that to the pan as well.

Cook on high heat until the curry comes to a boil, then reduce the heat, cover, and simmer for about 45 minutes. Check the curry from time to time and add a little extra cold water if it begins to dry out. Serve with Rotis (see page 28) or rice.

CHAAMP LAJAWAB
Spicy Lamb Chops

This recipe makes a wonderful main course, served with a mixed salad. The chops will be more tender if you marinate them overnight. In India, some cooks include a tablespoon of grated raw papaya in the marinade, as the enzyme papain helps to tenderize the meat. You can use either lamb rib chops or lamb loin chops for this recipe, but bear in mind that loin chops will take 3–4 minutes longer to cook on each side. These chops could also be cooked on a barbecue (wrap the bones in foil to prevent them from burning!).

Serves 4

8 lamb chops	1 teaspoon freshly crushed black pepper	1 teaspoon medium chili powder	2 teaspoons garam masala	¾ cup plain yogurt

Combine the chops, 3 teaspoons of Ginger-garlic Paste (see page 26), the black pepper, chili powder, garam masala, yogurt, and some salt in a mixing bowl, stirring to mix evenly. Cover and let marinate in the refrigerator overnight to allow the meat to absorb the flavors of the spices.

Preheat the broiler to medium-high.

Place the chops on the broiler rack over a pan and broil for 4–5 minutes on each side for medium-rare, or for 6–7 minutes on each side for well done.

Transfer the chops to a warm plate and let rest for 5–7 minutes before serving.

Serve with a mixed salad.

HARA JHINGA PULAO
Herby Green Rice with Shrimp

I always butterfly shrimp to enhance their juiciness and to get rid of the dark colored "vein" that runs along their back (see page 79). This vein is the shrimp's digestive tract, and I remove them because they can look unsightly, affect the taste of the dish, and I'd rather not eat the contents of a digestive tract. You can use smaller shrimp for this dish as they retain their moisture, but I'd still devein them. You can also substitute the jumbo shrimp with cubed chicken breast or thigh meat. I've given an option of 2–3 fresh green chilies, depending on whether you like a hotter or milder dish.

Serves 4

1 onion, sliced	2 handfuls of fresh cilantro	2 handfuls of mint, woody stalks discarded	2–3 fresh green chilies, roughly chopped (seeds and all)	1¼ cups basmati rice, washed and drained	7 ounces fresh raw jumbo shrimp, shelled, deveined, and butterflied (see page 79)	2 tablespoons fresh lemon juice

Heat 2 tablespoons of sunflower oil in a heavy-based saucepan and fry the onion on high heat for 3–4 minutes, until it starts to turn golden.

Meanwhile, tear the cilantro (leaves and stems) and the mint leaves into a blender. Add 2 teaspoons of Ginger-garlic Paste (see page 26) and the chilies and blend to as fine a paste as possible, adding scant 1 cup of cold water to turn the blades smoothly.

Add the rice to the onion, stir gently a few times to mix and then add scant 1 cup of boiling water. Stir in the green herby paste. Add the shrimp and season with salt, mixing lightly. Bring to a boil, then reduce the heat, cover, and simmer on the lowest setting for about 15 minutes, without lifting the lid. Turn off the heat and leave the pan covered for a further 5 minutes to finish cooking the rice in the steam.

Remove the lid and run a fork through the rice to loosen it. Serve the rice mixture hot, drizzled with the lemon juice.

MEEN MOLEE
South Indian Fish Curry with Coconut and Curry Leaves

This light fish curry is almost a stew, but unlike many southern dishes that are fiery hot, it's quite mild. Traditionally eaten with "appams" or fermented rice pancakes, I love it best with plain boiled rice with a dash of lemon juice squeezed on top. I use full-fat canned coconut milk as the reduced-fat one does not give this curry the creaminess it needs.

Serves 4

2 onions, finely chopped	2 fresh green chilies, finely chopped (seeds and all)	1 teaspoon ground turmeric	2 tomatoes, finely chopped (seeds and all)	4 firm skinless fish fillets, such as salmon, halibut, or cod loin	14-ounce can coconut milk	10 fresh or 15 dried curry leaves, chopped or crumbled

Heat 2 tablespoons of sunflower oil in a saucepan. Stir in the onions and cook for 4–5 minutes on high heat, until they start to brown, then reduce the heat and cook for a further 3–4 minutes, until they are soft.

Add 2 teaspoons of Ginger-garlic Paste (see page 26) and the chilies and cook for 30 seconds, until the raw garlic smell disappears, then add the turmeric and cook for a few seconds. Add the tomatoes and cook on high heat for 4–5 minutes, or until they soften and can be easily mashed with the back of a spoon.

Move the mixture to the sides of the pan and place the fish fillets in the center of the pan, adding a few extra drops of sunflower oil if the pan is too dry. Fry on both sides until well sealed and half cooked, about 2–3 minutes.

Pour in the coconut milk, add the curry leaves, and season with salt. Cook on low heat, covered, until the fish is tender, about 8 minutes.

Serve hot with plain boiled rice.

MURGH KA PULAO
Spiced Chicken Pulao

Serve this dish with a cucumber raita and you'll find that it becomes one of your go-to meals, as it is one of mine. You can use chicken on the bone—thighs are good—but cook them for a few minutes more than the breast meat. You can also throw in a handful of frozen diced mixed vegetables, such as carrots, green beans, and peas, to make this even healthier. The fried onions on top add a lovely sweet flavor. When I have the time, I often fry up a few onions until they are golden brown but not so dark that they taste bitter, and then freeze them to use later.

Serves 4

1 large onion, finely sliced	1 large tomato, finely chopped (seeds and all)	1 teaspoon ground turmeric	1 teaspoon medium chili powder	7 ounces skinless chicken breasts, cut into ¾-inch pieces	1¼ cups basmati rice, washed and drained	2 tablespoons fresh lemon juice

Heat 2 tablespoons of sunflower oil in a heavy-based saucepan. Fry the onion on high heat for 4–5 minutes, then remove half of the onion to a plate and set aside.

Fry the remaining onion in the pan on medium heat, stirring frequently, for a further 8–10 minutes, until dark golden in color. Drain on paper towels and set aside separately.

Put the first lot of onion back into the pan, turn up the heat to high, and add 2 teaspoons of Ginger-garlic Paste (see page 26). Fry for a few seconds, then add the tomato and cook for 1 minute. Sprinkle in the ground spices, mix, then add the chicken. Cook, stirring, until the chicken looks white instead of pink on the outside, about 3–4 minutes.

Now add the rice and 2 cups of boiling water and season with salt. Bring to a boil, then reduce the heat to its lowest setting, cover with a tight-fitting lid, and simmer for 12 minutes, without lifting the lid. Turn off the heat and leave the pan covered for a further 5 minutes to finish cooking the rice in the steam.

Remove the lid, add the lemon juice, and fluff up the rice with a fork. Sprinkle the reserved golden fried onions on top and serve hot with yogurt and cucumber.

KHEEMA PARATHA
Lamb-stuffed Flatbread

Although this looks a bit tedious when you first read the recipe, when you've made it a few times, you will realize how simple and delicious it is. I serve these parathas simply with some plain yogurt. Don't put too much ground meat mixture into each paratha, otherwise it becomes too heavy and unwieldy to flip over and can break. I choose ground lamb that contains around 10% fat, but you can use a lower-fat ground meat such as beef.

Makes 8 parathas

⚜	⚜	⚜	⚜	⚜	⚜	⚜
2 fresh green chilies, finely chopped (seeds and all)	½ teaspoon ground turmeric	1 teaspoon garam masala	7 ounces lean ground lamb	2 tablespoons finely chopped fresh cilantro leaves	3 cups stoneground wholewheat flour (atta)	tepid water

Heat 1 tablespoon of sunflower oil in a frying pan on high heat. Add 1 teaspoon of Ginger-garlic Paste (see page 26) and the chilies and cook for 1–2 minutes, until the mixture becomes aromatic. Add the spices and cook for a further minute.

Tip in the ground lamb and season with salt. Break up the meat with a wooden spoon, then cover and cook, reducing the heat when the mixture begins to bubble. Simmer for 15 minutes, or until the meat is cooked, then add the cilantro. Remove from the heat, carefully transfer the mixture to a blender or food-processor, and blend until quite smooth.

Meanwhile, make the dough. Put the flour (reserving a little for dusting) in a bowl with 1 tablespoon of sunflower oil and a large pinch of salt. Gradually stir in enough tepid water (about 1 cup) until you have a firm dough. Transfer the dough to a lightly floured work surface and knead well for 5–6 minutes, until smooth and no longer sticky.

Divide the dough into 16 equal-size balls. Roll each ball into a flat disk about 4 inches in diameter, dusting the dough with a little flour if sticky. Smear a layer of the ground lamb mixture over one disk of dough, then place another disk on top. Seal the edges together to form a flat package. Repeat with the remaining dough disks and lamb mixture to make the eight parathas. Transfer them to a piece of wax paper.

Heat a frying pan on high heat and dot it with 1 tablespoon of sunflower oil. Cook a paratha for 3–4 minutes on one side until flecked with tiny dark spots on the underside, then flip it over and cook on the other side for 3–4 minutes. Remove and keep warm, wrapped in foil, while you cook the remaining parathas in the same way. Serve hot.

VEGAN

BHOPLYACHI AMTI
Pumpkin in Coconut Milk

I love pumpkin and almost always cook it with the skin on. This adds a bit more texture to the dish and the skin softens enough upon cooking to chew easily. It also holds the shape of the pumpkin pieces and stops them from disintegrating. If the pumpkin is very fleshy, you'll have some pieces with no skin and they'll just collapse a bit more than the others. I've used strained tomatoes in this recipe, which give a smooth sauce when combined with the coconut milk. You can use roasted cashews for this recipe, or even add sunflower or pumpkin seeds instead, if you like.

Serves 4

☙	☙	☙	☙	☙	☙	☙
2 fresh green chilies, finely chopped (seeds and all)	10 fresh or 15 dried curry leaves, chopped or crumbled	1 teaspoon ground turmeric	scant 1 cup strained tomatoes	14 ounces seeded pumpkin, chopped into small cubes with the skin left on	14-ounce can coconut milk	15 unsalted cashews

Heat 2 tablespoons of sunflower oil in a saucepan. Stir in 2 teaspoons of Ginger-garlic Paste (see page 26) and the chilies and cook on high heat for a couple of minutes. Add the curry leaves and cook for a further minute, then add the turmeric and cook for a few seconds. Add the strained tomatoes and cook for 3–4 minutes, until everything is well blended.

Tip in the pumpkin, season with salt and then pour in scant ⅔ cup of boiling water. Bring to a boil, then reduce the heat, cover, and cook for 7–8 minutes, until the pumpkin is nearly tender, adding a few tablespoons of cold water if the pan starts to dry out.

Pour in the coconut milk, then stir in the cashews. Cook on medium heat until the curry comes to a boil.

Serve hot with poppadoms or plain boiled rice, if preferred.

PALAK AUR SOYA KI SUBZI
Spinach and Dill Curry with Tofu

Spinach and paneer are a classic combination in north Indian cuisine. The recipe also works well if you replace the paneer with tofu. From the three grades of tofu commonly available (firm, soft, and silken), I've used firm as it is closest in texture to paneer. Both paneer and tofu hold their shape and do not melt on cooking. I love the addition of dill leaves in this recipe—they add a unique flavor that complements the relatively mild flavor of spinach.

Serves 4

1 teaspoon cumin seeds	1 large onion, finely chopped	1–2 fresh green chilies, minced (seeds and all)	1 teaspoon garam masala	a large handful of dill, leaves picked (thick stems discarded) and chopped	1 pound fresh spinach, washed, drained, and finely chopped	8 ounces firm tofu, cubed and seasoned with a little salt

Warm 2 tablespoons of sunflower oil in a heavy-based saucepan and fry the cumin seeds until they turn dark. Add the onion and fry on high heat for 4–5 minutes, until it starts to turn brown, then reduce the heat and cook for a further 4 minutes.

Stir in 1 teaspoon of Ginger-garlic Paste (see page 26) and the chilies and cook for 30 seconds, then tip in the garam masala and cook for a few seconds. Add a splash of cold water and continue to cook on high heat until the water has evaporated.

Add the dill, spinach, and a little more salt and cook for a further 4–5 minutes. Reduce the heat to medium and continue cooking until the spinach leaves wilt completely and any liquid has evaporated. Fold in the tofu and heat through for 3–4 minutes until hot.

Serve hot with Rotis (see page 28).

GAJAR KOBI NU SHAK
Gujarati-style Carrot and Cabbage Stir-fry

Gujarati cooking is delicate, largely vegetarian, and full of unusual ingredients and combinations. Vegetables are not smothered in spices; instead they are lightly cooked with just a few spices that bring out their freshness and unique taste. There is not much use of dairy in main course dishes, except for a few curries made with yogurt. A combination of fresh green chilies and ginger is commonly used to flavor vegetable curries.

Serves 4

1 teaspoon black mustard seeds	2 fresh green chilies, slit in half lengthwise and stalks left on	1 teaspoon finely grated peeled fresh ginger	1 teaspoon ground turmeric	½ medium cabbage, finely shredded	2 large carrots, peeled and coarsely grated

Warm 2 tablespoons of sunflower oil in a heavy-based frying pan on high heat. Add the mustard seeds and wait until they pop, then add the chilies and ginger. Stir for a few seconds, then sprinkle in the turmeric and stir.

Add the cabbage and carrots, season with salt and stir to combine, then stir-fry on high heat for 3–4 minutes, until the vegetables start to soften.

Pour in 3–4 tablespoons of cold water. Bring to a boil, then reduce the heat, cover the pan, and cook for 10 minutes, or until the vegetables are cooked and the water has evaporated. If there is some water left at the bottom of the pan, cook, uncovered, on high heat for 2–3 minutes.

Serve hot with Rotis (see page 28).

ALOO MUTTAR MASALA
Potatoes and Peas with Cumin

Potatoes and peas are cooked together in various ways all over India. The addition of peanuts here adds a bit of texture and some protein to this dish. If you'd like a bit of crunch, add the peanuts at the end after the potatoes are cooked. I'm sometimes asked at my classes why the peas need to go in with the potatoes when they take less time to cook—I find that they still hold their shape but absorb the flavors better. You can use fresh peas when they are in season, but frozen ones work equally well.

Serves 4

1 teaspoon cumin seeds	2 fresh green chilies, slit in half lengthwise and stalks left on	2 tomatoes, finely chopped (seeds and all)	1 teaspoon ground turmeric	3 potatoes, peeled and cut into ½-inch cubes	¾ cup frozen garden peas	⅓ cup salted or unsalted peanuts

Warm 2 tablespoons of sunflower oil in a saucepan on high heat and add the cumin seeds. When they darken, add the chilies and fry for 10 seconds. Stir in the tomatoes and cook for 2–3 minutes, until soft. Tip in the turmeric and cook for a minute, still on high heat.

Add the potatoes and peas and enough hot water to just cover them. Sprinkle in the peanuts, then season with salt, using less if the peanuts you are using are salted ones. Bring to a boil, then reduce the heat and cook for 20 minutes, or until you can pierce a small knife through a cube of potato. The curry should have thickened because of the potatoes and not be watery.

Serve hot with Rotis (see page 28).

HYDERABADI BAINGAN

Hyderabad-style Sweet and Sour Eggplant

This is a twist on a dish from the former royal state of Hyderabad, situated in the central south of India. I first tasted it almost 25 years ago at a friend's home. It is quite an intensely flavored dish and goes well with boiled rice or rotis. Although the frying of the eggplant makes this dish rather rich, it is so delicious that I love it nevertheless. Drain the fried eggplant well on paper towels so that the final dish isn't oily.

Serves 4

2 tablespoons tamarind block	1 large eggplant, cubed	1 teaspoon ground turmeric	1 teaspoon medium chili powder	10 fresh or 15 dried curry leaves, chopped or crumbled	2 tablespoons soft brown cane sugar

Put the tamarind into a heatproof bowl, add ⅔ cup of warm water and mash together with your fingers until combined. Press the mixture through a fine-mesh strainer, then do another two pressings using scant ½ cup boiling water each time (see also page 12). Set the resulting tamarind pulp aside, and discard what's left in the strainer.

Heat enough sunflower oil in a deep frying pan that is large enough to hold the eggplant in a single layer (the oil should be about ½ inch deep). When it is almost smoking, reduce the heat to medium and fry the eggplant cubes quickly, in batches, until golden in color. It is important to have the oil really hot, otherwise the eggplant will need to remain in the oil longer and will needlessly absorb more oil. Remove from the heat and drain the eggplant cubes on paper towels.

Pour 2 tablespoons of the eggplant cooking oil into a separate frying pan, heat on medium heat, then add the ground spices. When they sizzle, add 2–3 tablespoons of cold water and bring to a boil. Add the curry leaves, then reduce the heat and cook until the water has evaporated.

Add the tamarind pulp and the sugar, then cook for a couple of minutes until the sugar has dissolved and you get a thick sauce. Add the fried eggplant cubes, season to taste with salt and cook for a further few minutes, mixing gently to combine them with the sauce.

Serve hot with plain boiled rice or Rotis (see page 28).

FARASBEAN BHAJI
Green Bean and Tomato Curry

Indian home-style cooking often features dishes like this one—where vegetables are cooked simply without too much spice and sauce. Green beans are commonly eaten all over India, where they are often referred to as French beans. One seldom sees this versatile vegetable on restaurant menus, though. You can buy trimmed beans or trim them yourself—simply cut off the ends and remove the strings from the sides. To grate a tomato, cut it in half and grate the cut sides on the large holes of a grater, discarding the skin.

Serves 4

☸	☸	☸	☸	☸	☸	☸
1 teaspoon black or brown mustard seeds	1 large onion, finely chopped	1 teaspoon ground turmeric	1 teaspoon medium chili powder	14 ounces green beans, chopped into ¾-inch pieces	2 ripe tomatoes, coarsely grated (and skin discarded)	2 tablespoons unsalted cashews

Warm 2 tablespoons of sunflower oil in a heavy-based frying pan on high heat and add the mustard seeds. When they pop, add the onion. Cook for 3–4 minutes (still on high heat), until the onion begins to change color, then reduce the heat and cook for a further 2–3 minutes, until soft.

Tip in the turmeric and chili powder and cook for a couple of minutes, then stir in the green beans. Pour in the tomatoes and season with salt.

Bring to a boil, then reduce the heat, cover, and simmer for 10 minutes, or until the beans are cooked. Add the cashews, remove from the heat, and serve hot.

ONION BHAJIA
Onion Fritters

These moreish fritters are commonly called "bhaji" outside of India, but in their native country a bhaji is a stir-fry of vegetables and not a fritter at all. Some Western chefs add egg to the batter—this is not necessary as the gram flour itself is sticky enough to be a binding agent. These gluten-free fritters are made from a particular variety of pulse called Bengal gram. Gram flour becomes crisp when fried and is therefore used in many Indian snacks including Bombay mix. Ajowan or ajowan seeds—also called carom seeds—are added to fritters, such as bhajia and pakoras, as such dishes, along with gram flour, can be heavy to digest, and ajwain seeds are known to be a digestive.

Serves 4

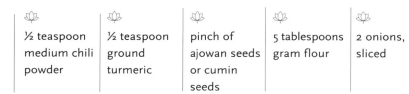

½ teaspoon medium chili powder	½ teaspoon ground turmeric	pinch of ajowan seeds or cumin seeds	5 tablespoons gram flour	2 onions, sliced

Combine the chili powder, turmeric, ajowan or cumin seeds, and gram flour in a mixing bowl. Pour in a little cold water at a time and mix to make a thick, custard-like batter. Season with salt, bearing in mind that you will need a little more than you think, as it will be seasoning the onions that go into the batter as well.

Heat enough sunflower oil (about ½ inch deep) in a large, deep frying pan on high heat until hot.

Fold the sliced onions, in batches, into the batter, evenly coating them with the batter. If you put all the onions into the batter at once, the salt in the batter will draw out the juice from the onions and make the batter loose. The batter should just coat the sliced onions.

Test the temperature of the oil by carefully dipping a slice of raw onion into it. The onion should immediately sizzle if the oil is hot enough.

Scoop up a tablespoon of the battered onions, drain off the excess batter on the side of the bowl and then drop the onions gently into the hot oil. Deep-fry in batches for around 2–3 minutes on each side, turning once, until golden and crispy. Remove using a slotted spoon and drain on paper towels. Wrap the fritters in foil to keep warm while you cook the remaining batter.

Deep-fry the remaining onions in the same way, bringing the oil back up to temperature before adding each batch. Serve hot.

CAULIFLOWER GASHI
Cauliflower in a Creamy Coconut Curry

My family has origins in the west coast of India, and in this region coconut forms the base for most dishes, so I grew up eating curries like this one. I sometimes add a big squeeze of lemon juice to this curry to intensify the flavors, but the creaminess of the coconut milk, the toasted earthiness of the dried shredded coconut and the sweetness of the onion perfectly complement the texture of the cauliflower. You can swap the cauliflower for potatoes and peas or carrots, if you like.

Serves 4

2 large onions, sliced	3 heaped tablespoons dried shredded coconut	½ cauliflower, cut into small florets	1 teaspoon Kashmiri chili powder	1 teaspoon ground turmeric	2 teaspoons garam masala	scant ½ cup coconut milk

Heat 1½ tablespoons of sunflower oil in a heavy-based frying pan and add the onions. Fry on high heat for 3–4 minutes, until they start to change color, then reduce the heat to medium and cook for a further 6–7 minutes, until they are soft and you can easily cut through a slice with the edge of a spoon. They should be light golden in color by now.

Add 2 teaspoons of Ginger-garlic Paste (see page 26) and cook for a few seconds. Add the dried shredded coconut and cook for 3–4 minutes, or until the mixture turns golden and the coconut develops a toasted fragrance.

Remove from the heat, carefully transfer the mixture to a blender, add enough cold water to just cover the mixture, then blend until well combined. Set aside.

Wipe the pan with a paper towel and then heat 1½ tablespoons of sunflower oil in it. Add the cauliflower and cook on high heat for 3–4 minutes, then add the chili powder, turmeric, and garam masala and season with salt. Mix well, add a couple of tablespoons of cold water and cook for a couple of minutes.

Tip in the curry sauce from the blender, mix, and then bring to a boil. Reduce the heat to medium, cover, and cook for 10–15 minutes, until the cauliflower has softened. Stir in the coconut milk, then heat through for a few minutes until hot.

Serve hot with plain boiled rice or couscous.

GUCCHI MUTTAR KA KORMA
Mushroom and Pea Korma

A curry-house korma in the UK has come to mean a mild creamy dish that is often sweetened with sugar. In India, a korma mostly has nuts as a base and can be hot or mild depending on where it comes from. I have given an option for the chilies—two for a milder curry and three if you like it hotter. The blending of the cashews in this recipe makes the curry creamy, but if you want a smoother sauce, you can add 3 tablespoons of oat cream or coconut cream at the end, just before taking the curry off the heat.

Serves 4

1 large onion, sliced	2–3 fresh green chilies, finely chopped (seeds and all)	scant ½ cup cashews	14 ounces mushrooms, cleaned and sliced	¾ cup frozen garden peas	1 teaspoon ground cumin	1 teaspoon garam masala

Put the onion, chilies, and cashews in a heavy-based saucepan with just enough cold water to cover. Bring to a boil, then reduce the heat and simmer for about 10 minutes, until the onion is soft enough to cut through a slice easily with the edge of a spoon.

Remove from the heat, then carefully transfer the mixture to a blender and add a little more cold water if needed, so the onion, chilies, and cashews are just covered. Blend to a puree, then set aside.

Heat 2 tablespoons of sunflower oil in a separate heavy-based saucepan on high heat. Add 2 teaspoons of Ginger-garlic Paste (see page 26) and cook for a few seconds, then add the mushrooms and peas, mix well, and fry for a minute. Stir in the ground spices and cook for a couple of minutes.

Add the sauce from the blender, then rinse the blender out with 2–3 tablespoons of cold water, and add that to the pan as well. Season with salt.

Bring to a boil, then reduce the heat and simmer for 7–8 minutes, covered, until the peas are soft.

Serve hot with Rotis (see page 28) or plain boiled rice.

MOSARU VADA
Lentil and Vegetable Fritters in Soy Yogurt

These south Indian lentil fritters are made even more delicious by the addition of vegetables—I've added fresh spinach, but you can also try using finely grated carrot. I like the fritters to be slightly crisp in the yogurt, so I add them just before serving. If you want them soft, dip them in water, squeeze them out, and then add them to the yogurt, or left long enough, they will soften in the yogurt. You could also add a sprinkling of chopped fresh cilantro leaves on top for a bit of color.

Serves 4

✿	✿	✿	✿	✿	✿	✿
scant 1 cup split white urid lentils, washed and drained	a handful of fresh spinach, washed, drained, and finely chopped	1⅓ cups plain soy yogurt	2 teaspoons white caster sugar	1 teaspoon black mustard seeds	1 teaspoon cumin seeds	3 large dried red chilies, broken in half, and seeds shaken out

Soak the lentils in a heatproof bowl with plenty of hot water for at least an hour. Drain off the water and then transfer the lentils to a blender with the spinach, adding enough cold water to almost but not quite cover the lentils and spinach. Blend until smooth—the result should be a smooth paste with no grains in it, the consistency of thick custard (you will need to add enough water to allow the blades of the blender to turn smoothly). Season with salt and set aside.

Heat enough sunflower oil in a deep frying pan (big enough to hold a single layer of fritters) on high heat. When the oil is almost smoking, carefully drop in a tiny ball of the lentil batter—it should quickly rise to the top.

Reduce the heat slightly and gently drop a few tablespoons of the batter into the oil. Flip them over a few times to color them evenly during cooking—they should be golden brown all over. When cooked (after 4–5 minutes), remove the fritters using a slotted spoon and drain them on paper towels. Deep-fry the remaining fritter batter in batches in the same way.

Meanwhile, in a separate large, heatproof bowl, whisk together the yogurt and sugar and season to taste with salt.

Heat 1 tablespoon of sunflower oil in a small saucepan and fry the mustard seeds until they pop. Add the cumin seeds and dried red chilies and then pour this tempering, along with the oil, over the seasoned yogurt. Just before serving, add the cool fritters to the yogurt. Serve cool.

TARKA DAL
Lentils with Tomatoes and Cilantro

There are many versions of this north Indian recipe, as the name literally means
"spiced, flavored lentils." There are several Indian words that describe the process
of tempering foods, including "tarka," "tadka," "vaghaar," or "phodni." Spices
or ingredients, such as tomatoes, garlic, ginger, or chilies, are cooked in hot oil
to extract and develop their flavor. Tempering can be done at the beginning of
cooking, where for example, spices and onions are cooked before adding the main
ingredient, or at the end, when for example, cumin seeds may be fried in oil and
poured over a curry. The oil contains the aromatic oils extracted from the spices
and becomes "flavored" itself.

Serves 4

1 cup mung (moong) lentils	1 teaspoon cumin seeds	2 fresh green chilies, slit in half lengthwise and stalks left on	2 tomatoes, diced (seeds and all)	1 teaspoon ground turmeric	1 teaspoon garam masala	a handful of fresh cilantro leaves, chopped

Wash the lentils in a strainer under running cold water until the water runs clear. Put
them into a heavy-based saucepan and then pour double the quantity of boiling
water over them (don't salt the lentils at this stage, as they can take longer to cook if
you do).

Bring to a boil, then reduce the heat and simmer until very soft, about 30 minutes,
adding more boiling water as they absorb what's in the pan. Ensure that the lentils
are submerged at all times. When the lentils are cooked, they should have completely
disintegrated and resemble oatmeal.

Meanwhile, warm 2 tablespoons of sunflower oil in a separate saucepan on high
heat and add the cumin seeds. As they begin to crackle and change color, add
1 teaspoon of Ginger-garlic Paste (see page 26) and cook for 30 seconds, then
add the chilies and cook for a further few seconds. Tip in the tomatoes and cook
for 3–4 minutes, until soft. Stir in the turmeric and garam masala, add a little cold
water and bring to a bubble.

Carefully pour in the cooked lentils, along with all the cooking liquid (no need to
drain) and season with salt. The mixture should have a pouring consistency.

Sprinkle the cilantro over, and serve hot with plain boiled rice or Rotis (see
page 28).

CHANNA MASALA
Chickpeas in a Spiced Curry Sauce

This simple recipe is one of the most popular ones at my cooking classes. You can make the curry sauce in bulk and freeze some, so that the next time it will take less than 10 minutes to make this curry. If you cook rice on the side and prepare a crisp salad, a hearty meal can be on the table within 20 minutes.

You can use other canned beans here—try lima or red kidney beans. The curry sauce can also be cooked with firm vegetables, such as potatoes, cauliflower, or broccoli—these will go into the pan first, then the ground spices along with a splash of water, and lastly, the curry sauce can be poured on top and cooked until the vegetables are tender. The blended sauce has a creamy consistency without the need to add any cream.

Serves 4

2 onions, sliced	1 tablespoon tomato paste	1 teaspoon ground turmeric	1 teaspoon medium chili powder	1 teaspoon ground coriander	14-ounce can chickpeas, drained and rinsed	2 tablespoons chopped fresh cilantro leaves, to garnish

Heat 1½ tablespoons of sunflower oil in a heavy-based saucepan and fry the onions on high heat for 4–5 minutes, until they start to turn golden brown. Reduce the heat to medium and cook for a further 7–8 minutes, until they are soft.

Add 1 tablespoon of Ginger-garlic Paste (see page 26) and cook for a few seconds, then add the tomato paste and fry for a minute, or until well blended.

Remove from the heat, carefully transfer the mixture to a blender, and add enough cold water to just cover the mixture, then blend until smooth. Set aside.

Heat 1½ tablespoons of sunflower oil in the same pan and add the ground spices. Fry on high heat for a few seconds, until they change color, then add 3–4 tablespoons of cold water and continue to cook until the water has evaporated, leaving the cooked spices in oil.

Add the chickpeas and mix well, then cook on high heat for 3–4 minutes, until the chickpeas have heated through.

Stir in the sauce from the blender and season with salt. Rinse out the blender with 2–3 tablespoons of cold water and add this to the pan as well. Bring to a boil, then reduce the heat, cover, and simmer for 5–6 minutes, until heated through. Garnish with cilantro and serve hot with plain boiled rice and Rotis (see page 28).

SWEET

AAM KA CAKE
Mango and Pistachio Mug Cakes

Although I am not a fan of microwave cooking, this recipe is a once-in-a-while treat that's really easy to make. I have made it with mango jam found in Indian stores, but this is not always easy to find and mango puree works equally well. I like mango puree from Indian Alphonso mangoes—it is fragrant, a rich saffron color, and very sweet. You can use the remainder of the can to make mango lassi—simply combine 3 tablespoons of mango puree with 4 tablespoons of plain yogurt and mix until well blended. You may want to add sugar to taste and a couple of pods of cardamom (use the seeds, crushed, and discard the husks).

Serves 4

⚘	⚘	⚘	⚘	⚘	⚘	⚘
⅓ cup salted butter	2 large free-range eggs, beaten	6 tablespoons soft brown cane sugar	¾ cup ground almonds	9 tablespoons (scant ½ cup) self-rising flour	4 tablespoons canned mango puree	2 tablespoons chopped pistachios

Melt the butter in a small saucepan, pour into a mixing bowl, then let cool. Add the eggs and sugar and beat until the sugar has dissolved. Fold in the almonds and flour.

Put a teaspoon of the mango puree into the bottom of each of four 10-ounce microwaveable mugs, then divide half of the cake mixture among them. Add the remaining mango puree (2 teaspoons into each mug), then top with the remaining cake mixture, spreading it level. Ensure that the mixture does not come more than three-quarters of the way up inside the mugs, as it will rise on cooking. Scatter the pistachios over the top.

Cook two mugs at a time in the microwave oven. Cook on full power/high (900 watts) for 3 minutes, or until risen and a skewer inserted into the middle of each cake comes out clean. Remove from the microwave, then cook the remaining two cakes in the same way.

Leave the cakes to stand for 10 minutes and then serve warm.

FRUIT SHRIKHAND TARTS
Fruit Yogurt Tarts with Cardamom, Pistachio, and Pomegranate

Shrikhand or hung yogurt, mixed with sugar, spices, and nuts, is a dessert served at festive times in the western states of Maharashtra and Gujarat. I've used the recipe to fill tart shells and create a pretty dessert. I often use mango yogurt and add some mango puree to it after it has drained for more intensity.

Makes 8 tarts or 18 mini tarts

⚜	⚜	⚜	⚜	⚜	⚜	⚜
4 cups whole-milk fruit yogurt (choose mango, strawberry, passion fruit, raspberry, or a mixed fruit one)	2 teaspoons fresh lemon juice	4 green cardamom pods, seeds crushed and husks discarded	pinch of ground nutmeg	8 ready-made (baked) individual sweet shortcrust pastry tart shells (each about 3 inches in diameter) or 18 mini tart shells (each about 1½ inches in diameter)	a few pistachios, crushed	a few pomegranate seeds

Tie the yogurt in a clean piece of cheesecloth and hang up to drain off the whey. I usually do this over the kitchen sink (or you can do it over a mixing bowl) for a minimum of 5 hours, or overnight.

When the yogurt is quite dense, scoop it out of the cheesecloth and place in a bowl along with the lemon juice. Beat well with a wooden spoon or whisk, adding the cardamom seeds and nutmeg.

When the yogurt is light and fluffy in texture, spoon it into the tart shells, dividing it evenly between them, and decorate with the pistachios and pomegranate seeds. Serve at once.

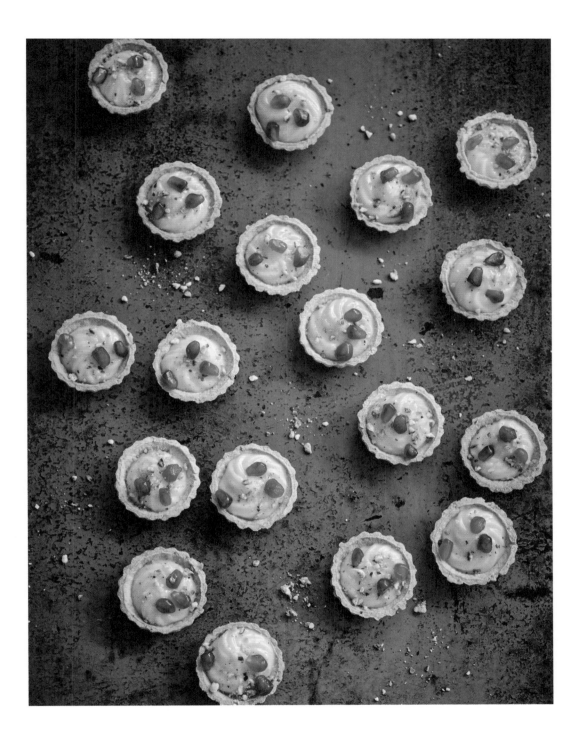

CHUKANDAR KA HALWA
Indian Beet Pudding

A halwa (halva) in India is a dessert, usually made with fresh or dried fruit, nuts, or grains and flavored with spices. Carrot halwa is popular, but beets grow plentifully and make a lovely rich, colorful dessert. You can use cooked beet here—you will need less milk, around a cup or less, as the cooking time to get the beet to become mushy will be much less.

Serves 4

⚘	⚘	⚘	⚘	⚘	⚘
1 tablespoon unsalted cashews, roughly broken	2 tablespoons ghee or salted butter	3 raw beets, peeled and coarsely grated	1¼ cups whole milk	½ cup white superfine sugar, or to taste	10 green cardamom pods, seeds crushed and husks discarded

Toast the cashews in a dry frying pan on high heat for 1–2 minutes, then tip on to a plate and set aside.

Heat the ghee or butter in a heavy-based saucepan until melted, then fry the beet on high heat for 3–4 minutes, stirring occasionally to prevent any sticking.

Pour in the milk and cook until the beet is mushy and the milk has been soaked up, about 40 minutes. The ghee should begin to separate at the edges at this point.

Stir in the sugar and continue to cook until the mixture is thick and jam-like, about 10 minutes, stirring from time to time. Add a pinch of salt (if using ghee rather than salted butter) and then mix in the crushed cardamom seeds.

Spoon into serving bowls, scatter over the toasted cashews, and serve warm with crème fraîche or yogurt.

KAALE CHAVAL KI PHIRNI
Black Rice Pudding

On one of my trips to India, I was given a small bag of Chak-hao or Manipuri black rice—Manipur is a state in the northeast of India, and this rice is also called purple rice or forbidden rice. It's very high in anthocyanins. The Manipuri people cook it into a festive rice pudding, so that was what I made in my own kitchen. The dazzling, deep-purple color, nutty taste, and creamy consistency were a delight, and back in London, I have made this recipe many times over using the more readily available Thai black rice.

Serves 4

⚜	⚜	⚜	⚜	⚜
⅓ cup black rice, washed and drained	generous 2 cups whole milk	3 tablespoons soft brown cane sugar, or to taste	5 green cardamom pods, seeds crushed and husks discarded	4 teaspoons sliced almonds

Put the rice into a blender with just enough milk to cover it and blend to a coarse paste. Set aside.

Heat the remaining milk in a saucepan on high heat. When it almost comes to a boil, reduce the heat to low and tip in the rice paste from the blender. Rinse the blender out with 3–4 tablespoons of cold water and pour this into the pan as well. Mix well and cook on high heat, stirring frequently, so that the rice does not stick to the bottom of the pan. Reduce the heat and continue cooking, stirring frequently, for 30–35 minutes, until the milk begins to thicken and the rice softens. Bear in mind that the pudding will set when it is completely cold and that the rice, even when cooked, will have a slightly chewy texture.

Remove from the heat and stir in the sugar, cardamom seeds, and half of the almonds. Mix well and then pour into individual serving bowls. Let cool, then chill in the refrigerator until set, about 2 hours.

Toast the remaining almonds in a small dry frying pan on high heat until they turn light golden in color, about 30 seconds. Remove from the heat and scatter the toasted almonds over the puddings just before serving.

Serve the rice puddings cold.

PARSI PUDDING
Indian Bread Pudding

The Irani Zoroastrian immigrants who came to India from Iran several hundred years ago brought with them a special cuisine that is much-loved in the cities where they set up small restaurants. This pudding is always on the menu in Irani cafés and has many versions—some with small charoli (chironji) nuts, others with caramel, but they are sold in small squares and can be eaten on the premises or taken away. The arrival of other cultures into India over many centuries has meant that the native cuisine has been able to absorb world culinary influences seamlessly.

Serves 4

5 slices of white or brown bread, crumbled or cut into small pieces	2 large free-range eggs, beaten	scant 1 cup whole milk	5 tablespoons white caster sugar	2 tablespoons unsalted cashews, chopped	5 green cardamom pods, seeds crushed and husks discarded	1 teaspoon vanilla extract

Preheat the oven to 400°F.

Put the bread into a large mixing bowl. In a separate bowl or pitcher, beat the eggs, then add the milk, sugar, cashews, cardamom seeds, and vanilla extract and mix well until the sugar has completely dissolved.

Pour this mixture over the bread. Press the bread down with the back of a spoon and leave it to soak for 5 minutes. Mix well, then pour this mixture into a baking dish and press down with the back of a spoon to flatten the top.

Bake in the oven for 30 minutes, or until a skewer inserted into the center comes out clean.

Serve hot or cold, cut into 4 x 1½-inch squares.

TIPS ⌣

You can also steam this pudding: put the bread mixture into a heatproof dish, cover with foil, and transfer to a steamer placed over a saucepan of simmering water. Cover with the lid and steam for 30–40 minutes, until a skewer inserted into the center of the pudding comes out clean.

Once the pudding is baked, you can make a caramelized sugar crust by sprinkling a layer of sugar on top, then putting the pudding under a preheated hot broiler for a few minutes until golden.

NANKHATAI
Indian Butter Cookies

The word "nankhatai" comes from two words: "naan" or leavened bread and "khatai," which is Afghani for biscuit. According to historians, these shortbread cookies originated in Surat, a town in western India where a Dutch couple ran a bakery serving Dutch traders. They then sold the bakery to an Indian baker who changed the recipe to omit eggs and make the cookies suitable for Indian vegetarian customers.

My grandmother was an exceptional nankhatai maker and I remember her baking these for us as a teatime snack when we got home from school. They were crisp and crumbly with a melt-in-the-mouth texture that made them completely irresistible. There are several recipes for these cookies—I add a bit of gram flour and semolina for crispness.

Makes 15 cookies

1 cup all-purpose flour	scant ½ cup gram flour	scant ¼ cup fine semolina	9 tablespoons (about ½ cup) powdered sugar	1 teaspoon ground cardamom	½ cup ghee or unsalted butter	2 tablespoons mixed pistachios and almonds, crushed or very finely chopped

Preheat the oven to 300°F. Line a baking sheet with wax paper.

Put the all-purpose flour, gram flour, semolina, powdered sugar, cardamom, and a large pinch of salt into a large mixing bowl and mix well. Rub in the ghee or butter to make a stiff dough. Refrigerate, covered, for 15 minutes.

Divide the dough into 15 equal portions, each about 1¼ inches in diameter. Shape each portion into a flat, round shape and place on the prepared baking sheet.

Press an indent in the top of each round with your finger and fill with chopped nuts. Press them down slightly into the dough.

Bake in the oven for 20 minutes, or until cracks appear on the top of each cookie. Transfer to a wire rack and let cool. The cookies will be soft as they come out of the oven but will crisp up as they cool. When completely cool, store in an airtight container and consume within a week.

CHOCOLATE LADDOOS
Chocolate and Milk Balls

Laddoos are a traditional Indian sweet, often made with flour, milk, nuts, and fruit, and spices such as saffron and cardamom. They are eaten on festive days, such as Diwali, the Hindu festival of light. Many people outside of India are not aware that chocolate forms a part of Indian dessert-making. I like using dark cocoa powder for this recipe as it gives a more intense color and taste, but you can use any cocoa powder that is chocolaty in taste.

Makes 20 laddoos

2 tablespoons salted butter, plus extra for greasing	14-ounce can sweetened condensed milk	1 cup cocoa powder	5 tablespoons chopped cashews or almonds	2 tablespoons dried shredded coconut

Put the butter and condensed milk into a heavy-based saucepan. Cook on low heat for about 10 minutes, stirring constantly, until the mixture thickens and begins to leave the sides of the pan.

Mix in the cocoa powder, stirring to remove any lumps, and make a smooth paste, then stir in half of the cashews or almonds.

Grease a baking dish with a little extra butter, then pour in the thick cocoa mixture and smooth the surface with a spatula. Let cool and set at room temperature.

Break off small pieces of the set mixture and roll each piece into a cherry-size ball. Dip some of the chocolate balls in the remaining chopped cashews or almonds and some in the shredded coconut until coated, leaving some plain, too, so that you have a mix of textured laddoos.

Store in an airtight container in the refrigerator for up to a week.

CHINA GRASS

Milk and Cardamom Vegetarian Jello

This dessert was a childhood favorite of mine—we often had it at home during the hot summers, as it was so easy to make and because some of my family were vegetarian and did not eat animal gelatin. You can flavor it with any number of dessert flavorings, such as rosewater, nutmeg, and cocoa powder.

Agar-agar is a vegetarian gelling agent made from red algae, with no smell or color. It has been used in Indian vegetarian cooking for many years due to its non-animal origins and because it has a high setting point, which means it will set even at room temperature in a tropical country. It can be bought as strands, powder, or flakes, and can usually be found in the world food section of supermarkets and grocery stores.

Serves 4

1 teaspoon agar-agar flakes or powder, or ¼ ounce agar-agar strands	generous 2 cups whole milk	½ cup caster sugar	5 green cardamom pods, seeds crushed and husks discarded	2 teaspoons finely chopped or crushed mixed almonds and pistachios

Put the agar-agar into a heavy-based saucepan along with scant ½ cup of cold water and mix well. Bring to a boil, stirring so that it does not stick to the bottom of the pan. Reduce the heat and cook gently for 7–8 minutes, stirring, until the agar-agar has completely dissolved.

Combine the milk and sugar in a separate heavy-based saucepan and bring to a boil on high heat, stirring frequently so that it does not catch on the bottom of the pan. Reduce the heat and simmer for 3–4 minutes, stirring, until the sugar has dissolved.

Pour the sweetened hot milk into the dissolved agar-agar mixture and mix well for a couple of minutes. Strain this through a fine-mesh strainer into a heatproof bowl, then stir in the cardamom seeds.

Transfer the mixture to a heatproof serving dish and let cool at room temperature. Once cool, transfer to the refrigerator to finish setting, about 45 minutes.

When you are ready to serve, sprinkle with the chopped or crushed nuts and serve cold.

BHAPA DHOI
Steamed Sweet Yogurt

Yogurt is an essential ingredient in Indian cuisine and almost all Indian homes make their own. It is only recently that yogurt has become available in cartons. This Bengali dessert is simple to make and can be served on its own or with fruit. I use a mixture of finely crushed pistachios and almonds, to give texture and color to this dessert.

Serves 4

1 cup Greek yogurt	scant ⅔ cup sweetened condensed milk	6 green cardamom pods, seeds crushed and husks discarded	3 teaspoons chopped mixed nuts and raisins

Put the yogurt and condensed milk in a mixing bowl and whisk to make a smooth, lump-free mixture. Add the cardamom seeds and half of the mixed nuts and raisins and mix well. Pour into four individual molds or ramekins (about 6 tablespoons each), then cover each one with foil and seal.

Transfer the molds/ramekins to a steamer placed over a saucepan of simmering water, cover with the lid, and steam for 15 minutes. Alternatively, you can put the molds/ramekins into a deep baking pan, then fill the pan with enough boiling water to come halfway up the sides of the molds/ramekins (known as a bain-marie) and bake in a preheated oven at 350°F for 20 minutes, or until the yogurt is set but still slightly wobbly.

Remove the molds/ramekins from the steamer or bain-marie and let cool, then chill in the refrigerator for at least 4 hours before serving.

Serve cold, sprinkled with the remaining mixed nuts and raisins.

SANTRE KA SHEERA
Orange and Semolina Pudding with Saffron

One of my favorite desserts, semolina pudding in India is nothing like the semolina pudding most English schools used to serve with a spoonful of jam on the top. This Indian pudding, called "sheera," "halwa," or "rawa," is fragrant with spices and is fluffy and creamy at the same time. I've combined it with oranges here, but it can also be made with mashed banana or finely diced pineapple. The semolina is dry-roasted toward the start of the cooking process to bring out its nutty flavor.

Serves 4

⚜	⚜	⚜	⚜	⚜	⚜
2 sweet oranges	½ cup soft brown cane sugar	large pinch of saffron threads	4 green cardamom pods, seeds crushed and husks discarded	1 cup plus 2 tablespoons semolina	3 tablespoons ghee or unsalted butter

Grate the zest from the oranges, then peel the fruit, removing the pith, and roughly chop the flesh. Set aside.

Mix the sugar with 1¼ cups of cold water in a saucepan and bring to a boil. When the sugar has dissolved, add the orange zest, chopped orange flesh, saffron, and cardamom seeds and stir. Remove from the heat.

Meanwhile, put the semolina into a dry heavy-based frying pan and dry-roast on high heat for 5–6 minutes, stirring frequently, until it develops a nutty aroma and starts to turn slightly golden in color. Add the ghee or butter and continue to cook for a couple of minutes.

Reduce the heat, then carefully pour the orange mixture into the semolina, standing back from the pan as the mixture will splutter. Cook on low heat, stirring, until the liquid has been absorbed completely and the mixture is dry and fluffy, about 3–4 minutes.

Fluff up with a fork and serve warm.

INDEX

ACKNOWLEDGMENTS

I owe big thanks to several people who made this book possible—my children Arrush and India who made valuable contributions to our discussions on how busy, young people of today eat, to Bob for being lovely and being my chief taster, to Kyle Books for commissioning me to write another book. To Vicky Orchard, my editor, for her command over the entire book creating process and to the editorial and design team for creating such a beautiful book, especially to Gareth Morgans for his superb photography and to Sunil Vijayakar for the food styling (and to their teams – what fun we had in the photo studio!!!).